21:00   HV

D0253297

BLESSED ARE THE POOR?

EDITORIAL BOARD

James A. Nash, Chair
Churches' Center for Theology and Public Policy

Karen Bloomquist
Commission for Church in Society,
Evangelical Lutheran Church in America

Daniel Rush Finn
St. John's Seminary (Collegeville, MN)

Alan Geyer
Wesley Theological Seminary

Patricia Beattie Jung
Wartburg Theological Seminary

Peter J. Paris
Princeton Theological Seminary

Larry L. Rasmussen
Union Theological Seminary (New York)

J. Deotis Roberts
Eastern Baptist Theological Seminary

Thomas Shannon
Worcester Polytechnic University

Charles C. West
Princeton Theological Seminary

J. Philip Wogaman
Wesley Theological Seminary

BLESSED ARE THE POOR?

Women's Poverty, Family Policy, and Practical Theology

PAMELA D. COUTURE

Colorado Christian University
Library
180 S. Garrison
Lakewood, Colorado 80226

ABINGDON PRESS
Nashville

in cooperation with

THE CHURCHES' CENTER
FOR THEOLOGY AND PUBLIC POLICY
Washington, D.C.

BLESSED ARE THE POOR?
WOMEN'S POVERTY, FAMILY POLICY,
AND PRACTICAL THEOLOGY

Copyright © 1991 by Abingdon Press

All rights reserved.
No part of this work may be reproduced or transmitted in any form or by any means, electronic or mechanical, including photocopying and recording, or by any information storage or retrieval system, except as may be expressly permitted by the 1976 Copyright Act or in writing from the publisher. Requests for permission should be addressed in writing to Abingdon Press, 201 Eighth Avenue South, Nashville, TN 37203, U.S.A.

Library of Congress Cataloging-in-Publication Data

Couture, Pamela D., 1951–
    Blessed are the poor? : women's poverty, family policy, and practical theology / Pamela D. Couture.
        p. cm.
    Includes bibliographical references and index.
    ISBN 0-687-03615-1 (alk. paper)
    1. Poor women-United States. 2. Family policy-United States. 3. Women heads of households-United States. 4. Theology, Practical. I. Churches' Center for Theology and Public Policy (Washington, D.C.) II. Title.
HV1445.C68   1991   362.82′94575′0973-dc20   91-15985

97 98 99 00 01 02 03 04 — 10 9 8 7 6 5 4

For my mother, Barbara,
and her parents, Paula and William Kelsall,
and for my father, James,
and his parents, Louise and Wilfred (Pete) Couture
whose civic, domestic, and ecclesial values
infuse this work.

TABLE OF CONTENTS

ACKNOWLEDGMENTS

As I have written this book I have delighted in remembering the people who helped to form my convictions and approach to this subject. In my undergraduate years Marjorie Dew sparked my initial interest in American Studies; in seminary I experienced the empowering influence of the recovery of women's traditions through the work of Rosemary Skinner Keller and Rosemary Radford Ruether. While my mother modeled domesticity but always encouraged my entrance into public vocation, Rosemary Keller provided for me the vision of choosing domesticity in the midst of an increasingly public life.

The theological struggle which gave rise to this book began in the most unlikely of places. As I prepared for elders' orders in the United Methodist Church, I was informed that I was lacking one course. Protesting, I went back to seminary to take one more course in the theology of Wesley. During this course I became convinced that Wesley's doctrine of sanctification, which had been so appealing to women in the Wesleyan tradition, was fundamentally incompatible with domesticity. Since that time I have circled around the theologies of domesticity and self-sufficiency, at times not realizing that I was following many roads in pursuit of the same quest.

During this time I also came face to face with the legal adversary system when I divorced. The shock of putting dollars and cents on the contributions to a marriage left me with much to think about. The divorce also threw me back onto the mercy of the church if I was going to finish seminary or become a pastor. During this time many women, men, and youth at the First United Methodist Church of Arlington Heights, Illinois, and later, at Roselle United Methodist Church, not only helped, but *cared*, offering me and my children a rare combination of personal encouragement and practical support. So many cared that I am reluctant to single out any particular persons, but there are some who came forth in those years without whom this book would never have been written: Debbie Metz, Helen and Lloyd Cull, the Maschio family, Ian Evison and Leah Haworth, Cindy and Steve Simmons, Sharon Frank and Mark Conner, Mark Graham, and Lu Kness. They convinced me, irrevokably, about human interdependence within the grace of God. They revealed with unmistakable clarity the frequently invisible supports which anchor the flourishing of both children and adults.

After I decided to attend the University of Chicago in the new program in practical theology, I thought I had abandoned my scholarly interests in the family. I did not realize, when I wrote my first paper on self-sufficiency in Aristotle for Franklin I. Gamwell, that I was preparing to circle back to the same topic. However, encounters with single women, adolescents, and families during the years I served as a pastoral counselor at the Samaritan Center on the Ridge in Griffith, Indiana, put the issue of economics, interdependence, and the family back on the front burner with the heat turned up high. I had experienced the importance of support from the laity at the churches I had served, but now I frequently witnessed the problems created by the absence of support as people told me their sacred stories. Again, they taught me irrevokable lessons about the way that the breakdown of communities and families was creating a social situation which called for less, not more, demands for social self-sufficiency. If pastoral counseling could bring its insights into the world of social policy, it seemed to me that it would help to prevent, rather than only clean up after, the enormously difficult situations facing children and adults today. This conviction led me to a dissertation in public policy despite my emphasis in pastoral care.

Fortunately, my graduate program in practical theology at

the University of Chicago, guided by Don Browning, Robin Lovin, Anne Carr, and Martin Marty, allowed me to pursue these seemingly divergent social and personal interests while I immersed myself in the texts of the intellectual tradition. My colleagues at Candler School of Theology, Emory University—Rod Hunter, Chuck Gerkin, Rebecca Chopp, Steve Tipton, Chuck Foster, Jim Fowler, Bill Everett, Ad and John Carr, Ted Runyon, Noel Erskine, Fred Craddock, Roberta and Richard Bondi, and Wolfgang Huber—have shared information, read chapters, listened to ideas, read portions of the text, and otherwise provided the encouragement to me to complete this portion of this work. Equally important, the students in my classes, "Caring for Impoverished Children" and "Feminism, Psychoanalysis, and American Politics," at Chicago Theological Seminary and Candler School of Theology, refined my thinking and taught me the hermeneutics of making this work accessible for a wide range of people. Kathy Landin, Steve Simmons, and Greg Dell read portions of the manuscript with an eye to local church perspectives. Linda Tatro, Jan Tisdale-Edwards, Karen DeNicola, Barbara Ellwell, and Robin Stinson have helped to prepare the manuscript. My editor, Rex Matthews, patiently and carefully watched this project develop over a period of years, helped me to refine my ideas, and finally, took the risk of sponsoring the publication of a book whose author had not yet proven that she could transform her Chicagoese.

I have written this interdisciplinary book with the laity of all disciplines in mind, attempting to speak out—rather than up or down, as John Carr has called it—to all who might be interested in its argument. In an effort to make the text as accessible as possible, I have attempted to avoid or define the jargon of the various disciplines while maintaining the sophistication of the argument.

Even though I have drawn upon the work of people of color to critically modify and test my argument, I want to acknowledge that this book is written from my own perspective, that of a middle-class, white woman. In addition to my assumption that I can only write from my own social location,

I also suspect that a reflection on mothering from a middle-class white woman's perspective is necessary. Reflections on the experience of mothering may be more conflicted among middle-class white women than among women of color, for whom the role of mothering is largely a socially-prized role. I hope that the theoretical framework and solutions presented here suggest ways that commitments of mothering among middle-class white women and those held by women of color may share some common aims. Middle-class white women can learn much from the practices of women of color, but we must also be prepared to call upon portions of our own tradition which criticize dominant society. This work points toward those goals.

Finally, I thank my children and my husband. As this work has developed, my daughters Meredith and Shannon have been grown from toddlers into interesting young women in their own right. They patiently abide a mother who is calling in her chips: "I've listened to your reports for years; now what do you think of this?" They also continue to remind me that I am a mother as well as a teacher and writer. My husband, Carl Schneider, a divorce mediator and pastoral counselor, not only has encouraged me but has provided provocative information from his ever-expanding archives on family and the economics of divorce and his own practical experience. To them, and to the many other relatives and friends to whom I owe letters, I pledge that during Christmas next year, all I will write is Christmas cards.

Pamela D. Couture
Atlanta, 1991

FOREWORD

Pamela Couture's *Blessed Are the Poor?* is a convincing and provocative book about the realities of women's poverties and the possibilities of change. Couture combines rigorous scholarship, her own experiences of being a single mother and a minister, and keen insight about everyday life to portray the realities of women's poverties in the United States. (Readers may be surprised to discover that women's poverties are not the same problem in European countries as in the United States.) *Blessed Are the Poor?* reveals how we, as a culture, stubbornly cling to beliefs about self-sufficiency. Such clinging to hopeless myths entails a high cost—a cost of enormous physical, mental, and spiritual suffering—borne daily by the most vulnerable among us: children, single mothers, the poor.

By examining particular examples, cultural myths, media portraits, and statistics about women's poverties, Couture leads us through a complex maze of problems: the legal system, cultural values and beliefs, the rhetoric of equality, divorce reforms, economic practices. She is a wise and careful guide: beginning with an account of a film on homelessness and women that frames our own inability to know how to react to women's poverties, Couture teaches us to see and name the questions which we must learn to ask about the causes and prevention of such massive poverty.

If the text empowers our understanding of women's poverties and the tradition of self-sufficiency, it also provides resources for the transformation of women's poverties and for creating a new tradition of shared responsibility. From Martin

Luther, Couture draws resources for an ethic of domesticity; from John Wesley, she gleans suggestions for an economic ethic. These contribute to an ethic of care, which she traces through the American women's movement in the depth and breadth of all the ways in which mothers have struggled and persevered. The classical American tradition provides notions of interdependency which challenge the dominant mythology of self-sufficiency. Weaving these together, Couture envisions for us the values and policies of what a tradition of shared responsibility might mean in the United States.

Blessed Are the Poor? makes important contributions in a number of fields. In feminist theology, this book charts new territory by valuing the variety of women's traditions and the ways in which they contribute to the present situations of women while linking women to the experiences of past generations. In practical theology, Couture's work contributes methodologically an Aristotelian model of practical reflection around that which could be other and substantively a model of blending reflection on popular culture together with theoretical analysis. To the fields of public policy and the social sciences, this work will be important for suggesting the presence of theological values and for providing alternatives to the present values of self-sufficiency.

Blessed Are the Poor? models a new form of American public theology. The text speaks to American society—to all of us—about one of our most pressing problems. Daring to cross disciplinary lines, willing to bring together popular culture and scientific theories, Pamela Couture gets us to look at our life together and how all of us contribute to the suffering of those among us who are most vulnerable. In the rich tradition of American public theology, Couture addresses our problems and fuels our desires for new ways of forming our social order.

Rebecca S. Chopp
Candler School of Theology
Emory University

14

INTRODUCTION

The Authority of Practical Knowing

"God Bless the Children," a 1988 ABC special, featured a mother, Theresa Johnson, and her daughter, Hillary, struggling against the obstacles created by poverty. The Johnson family had come to the city looking for work, but Mr. Johnson deserted the family when he could not find stable employment. The film begins as Theresa and Hillary are evicted from their apartment building before it is razed in order to make way for a convention center. We follow them through their nights in shelters, Theresa's loss of her job, Hillary's withdrawal from school, their application for welfare, their weeks in tenement housing, and, finally, Hillary's bout with lead poisoning. The doctor warns Theresa that a new case of lead poisoning could leave Hillary with brain damage or learning disabilities. Above all, Theresa must not let the disease recur. In old buildings such as shelters, the doctor warns, lead was not only in the paint but "in the air." Defeated, loving her daughter but unable to protect her, Theresa decides to give Hillary up for adoption.

This special was aired at the height of discussion of a "feminization of poverty" in the U.S. During the 1980s the American public had become aware that poverty was increasing among children and their mothers more rapidly than among any other group. Some children, like Hillary, were becoming part of the growing population of homeless people in the U.S.; others remained in their homes but became deprived in relation to their neighbors. As the situation gained public and political attention, some analysts blamed trends in the general economy; others blamed the reallocation of entitlements from children to the elderly; others blamed no-fault divorce. Although they offered different explanations for the rise of female-headed households, analysts and the public now knew that the "female-headed household," single mothers and their children, were exceptionally vulnerable to poverty.

Concurrently, researchers for the Commission of the European Communities concluded that single mothers and their children were also the most economically vulnerable group in Europe. Their vulnerability, however, did not lead to a European "feminization of poverty." Some European countries had already developed universal family policies which protected against this vulnerability in a variety of ways, and other countries were prepared to adopt similar policies. Universal family policies, unlike welfare, provide a basic network of benefits for all families after which families with special needs gain special services. The European family policies were effective in a variety of different circumstances. The length of time the policies were in effect seemed to make no difference: Denmark had comprehensive family policies, including family allowances and child support, which dated from 1890; West Germany and Austria instituted family support policies in the 1980s. Women's employment patterns varied: family policies encouraged and enabled women to become employed, as in Sweden, or helped women with young children to remain in the home, as in the Netherlands. Family policies did not increase the number of female-headed households: the rate of single parenthood remained low—hovering around 11%—in most countries. Rates of single parenthood reached 30% in the United States, with few universalized family policies, and in Sweden, with the most comprehensive family policies. Family policies also did not encourage teen pregnancy. While adolescent pregnancy was a "former problem" in the European countries, only the United States had a significant group of teenage single mothers.[1]

As European countries increased their support for universalized family policies, the United States policy discussion was dominated by the idea that welfare breaks up the family and encourages "dependency." Therefore, argued Charles Murray in *Losing Ground: American Social Policy 1950–1980*, the U.S. should disband its welfare program entirely.[2] Eliminating welfare would encourage families to stay together, would force them to support one another, and would discourage out-of-wedlock pregnancy; in other words, families would take responsibility for one another. U.S. legislators were unwilling to go as far as Murray suggested; in fact, Murray himself later retreated from his position. But they were also unwilling to take their cues from the successful European system, despite the widespread support of these programs in major family research centers such as the University of Wisconsin, the Urban Institute, and the Kennedy School of Government, and despite the publicity given to these programs by legislators such as Pat Schroeder. The United States had been shown a successful method for eliminating poverty among children and their mothers, but in the 1980s American politicians' first priority was to eliminate "dependency" rather than to eliminate poverty. In order to discourage dependency, they called on the language of a long-standing American tradition: the tradition of self-sufficiency.

The language of self-sufficiency pervaded at least two movements for reform which have restructured the lives of parents and children in the U.S. in the last two decades. The first reform, the reform of laws governing divorce, began in California in the late 1960s and early 1970s and continues to proliferate in various forms of state legislation. The second reform, the reform of welfare, was enacted in 1988. In both reforms, the goal of individual "self-sufficiency" of the single parent household emerged as the norm of the day. "Self-sufficiency" meant the capacity of a single adult (male or female) household to provide for its dependents without help from society and often with little assistance from other family members.

This kind of self-sufficiency moved U.S. policy in the opposite direction from the successful European policy. As the language of self-sufficiency has become more and more dominant, the U.S. public has been willing to listen to forecasts that the United States is developing a "permanent underclass" and that large portions of today's generation of children will spend their early years in such deprivation that their futures will be seriously impaired. What is going on?

Social Science and Tradition

One might imagine that public policy makers objectively consider statistics—"the facts"—then make decisions based on proven data. Not so. Public policy makers use data to guide their decisions, but they shape those decisions within the contours of the political, economic, civil, and religious traditions which infuse our culture. Variations on the theme of self-sufficiency can be found in all of these traditions. Our political tradition holds almost sacred the belief in the autonomy of the family and the rights of the states to govern domestic law. Our economic tradition is built upon the freedom of the marketplace. Our civil tradition values the equal rights of all citizens. Our religious tradition, especially, values the worth of the individual and brings controversies over self-sufficiency into our historical consciousness. Our traditions also contain alternatives to self-sufficiency. In the present debate, policy makers have used particular sets of data in relation to the tradition of self-sufficiency to popularize the new reforms. Policy makers, however, rarely acknowledge the role of tradition in their decisions.

Average Americans are generally more comfortable with the beliefs derived from tradition than they are confident with the hard data which inform policy discussions. The "numbers" are formidable, and the "powers" who make policy seem so distant. Average Americans, therefore, tend to leave policy discussions to the thinktanks. Consider, for example, the reaction of my students to "God Bless the Children." An exceptionally well-crafted film, it introduces, in the story of one family and their acquaintances, the majority of issues which are found in the policy discussions of poverty of the

1980s. After my students viewed "God Bless the Children," I asked them to define the problem and offer a solution. Some students found the movie so upsetting they had to leave the room. They discovered powerful levels of compassion and empathy for Theresa and Hillary. Their religious concern was activated. Ultimately, they believed that under the reign of God, no child should suffer as Hillary did, and no mother should face such impossible odds as Theresa did. When they defined the problem, they gave the standard/traditional answers of sophisticated churchpeople, ranging from "all of the circumstances created a downward spiral" to "she didn't take advantage of all of the opportunities." But no one recognized the policy implications of the film: only one person mentioned that Theresa received no child support, and no one mentioned that in almost any other industrialized country, governmental policy would have provided Theresa and Hillary with the kind of basic support which would have allowed Theresa and Hillary to stay together. If policy makers tend to ignore tradition, churchpeople often fail to look closely enough at the specifics of concrete policy proposals.

Our tradition is as complex as social scientific data. At various times, some currents of tradition will be closer to the surface and will be easily called upon in debate, as the tradition of self-sufficiency is now; others are quiet and do not make their presence known as rapidly. Our traditions, therefore, can both comfort and challenge us. When we face a problem such as the growing poverty of women and children, we often feel helpless, as if the problem is too immense for us to do anything about. In those times, we use our traditions to make our leaders' decisions, especially their questionable ones, temporarily palatable. Inevitably, however, we also rely upon our traditions to give us a basic sense of what is good, right, or fair. Our traditions hold our ultimate commitments; therefore, the multiple currents of traditions also help us question political decisions which seem not to make sense.

The Crisis of Authority:
Why We Need Social Science and Tradition

The struggle of my class in responding to my questions about "God Bless the Children" demonstrates the way average citizens and churchpeople tend to avoid social science and public policy discussions, feeling overwhelmed by the complexity of data they have no way to evaluate. Politically, most people know that the systems of the world are complex, and they know that they are not the "experts." As religiously grounded people, however, they have convictions about the way a society should treat people and about the responsibilities a good person has toward society. Can they find a way to bring their convictions into dialogue with social science and culture?

The political science of democracy was built on the belief that an average man [sic] who has accurate information will make a reasonable political decision. What happens to democracy if the average person cannot get "the facts"? In a 1922 book entitled *Public Opinion*, Walter Lippmann described a U.S. in which the average person, through no fault of his or her own, could not get undistorted facts.[3] As an antidote to this problem, Lippmann predicted the rise of social science as public policy; in the future, Lippmann thought, the facts would be collected in large data banks which would be available to highly sophisticated think tanks, a social scientific elite who would have access to information which accurately described the U.S. and the world situation.

The problem to which Lippmann pointed was deeper than whether a citizen would have access to the facts. The kind of information to which Americans gave authority was changing. In previous centuries political or religious ideas had been given authority by the private citizen who, through local institutions such as the church, the school, the courthouse, or communications such as letters and visiting speakers, encountered the ideas of the day, discussed them with friends, and integrated new ideas into his or her own well of wisdom. A citizen nurtured his or her own authority by assimilating the intergenerational culture of his or her family or community and then joining in the creation of American tradition when new observations and situations called for new ideas.

Authority in 20th-century America, in contrast, has been conferred on scientific specialties. A mother, who may not have learned multiple models of psychology, has a gut sense that her child is in trouble. If she seeks help, she is faced with a proliferation of social-scientific decisions: for example, whether to read a self-help book, and if so, whether it should be about teenage development, family development, addiction, etc.; whether to seek the advice of a doctor: a family doctor, a psychiatrist, a psychologist, a psychotherapist, etc.; whether to seek testing: educational, organic, personality, etc. When she seeks professional help, her gut sense may easily be swept aside by the "helper's" wave of complicated data which is interpreted through professional jargon. She is immediately reminded that her gut sense does not have scientific validity. It has not been proven by scientific method. Yet the mother, and good scientists, know that her gut sense has authority. She has integrated a variety of traditions, many of which she cannot name, and has come to a conclusion that her child needs help. When faced with a conflict between scientific validity and cultural authority, she is forced to make what philosophers call an "epistemological" decision: what authority does she give to various kinds of knowledge? How does she weigh the authority of her own sense in relation to the data of hard science, such as testing, and the theories of soft science, such as personality theory?

I am not advocating that we abandon scientific inquiry. On the contrary, the doctor versed in personality theory can provide a kind of help for the child which was not easily available in past centuries. I am suggesting, however, that scientific authority has become scientific tyranny, just as, in previous centuries, religious and political authority became tyrannical. The religious and political innovators of previous times offered wisdom which could advance the cause of love and justice in previous cultures. Eventually, however, these authorities manipulated their power to serve the interests of a select group. Similarly, scientific knowledge can be used to create a better world and a better society. Scientific data can help to describe the world in a unique way. But scientific data, like other kinds of information, are limited. The methods, subjects, and organization of the research may lead to genuinely contradictory data; furthermore, these data are interpreted within one of many strands of tradition. Charles Murray, therefore, can limit his subject for research in a particular way and can interpret it within a particular strand of the tradition of self-sufficiency, and William Julius Wilson and Lenore Weitzman can organize their research in a different way and interpret their data within a different tradition. Given these limitations, the conclusions drawn by interpreters of social science must be in critical dialogue with a variety of cultural traditions which represent ultimate values and commitments. When this dialogue does not occur, scientific power may be used in the service of a few at the expense of many. To guard against such tyranny, "practical knowing," which sifts social scientific data through the sieve of our religious, political, and philosophic cultural traditions and vice versa, helps the average citizen make informed decisions.

The mother's gut sense, as she makes a decision about help for her child, is formed by her practical knowing. As she takes into account her observations of her child, the traditions of mothering, and the feedback she hears from the specialists, she will implicitly or explicitly answer three questions: what motivates human beings to do good? what does society owe her child, and what does her child owe society? are human beings and society accountable to anything beyond themselves? If she believes that human beings are basically good, she will be inclined to accept help from many sources. If she believes that society owes her child nothing, she will not think to ask whether there are sources of help in the school or public health department. If she believes that she is accountable for her child's welfare to a transcendent, life-giving power, her gut sense may override the obstacles in individuals and social service systems which block her efforts to get help for her child. The answers to these questions, and the way they shape human thought and behavior, have been the debated over many centuries by philosophers, politicians, and theologians. Every mother is a philosopher; every mother is a politician; every mother is a theologian.

Practical Theology
and the Debate about the Family

Practical theology is informed by practical knowing. As a theological discipline, practical theology represents a more formalized version of the thinking process through which an average person attempts to bring social science, cultural traditions, and religious convictions into dialogue with one another. Practical theology currently has many definitions. In this work, and in much of the most current discussion on practical theology, "practical" means reflection on practices, habits and situations. This definition of "practical" incorporates the three historical meanings of the word: practical as political, as personal, as technological.[4] "Theology" refers to claims about the divine-human and human-human relationships which express our ultimate commitments; as such, theology can be understood as explicit theological reflection. Ultimate assumptions also may be embedded in writing which does not make explicit theological claims. Many religious assumptions are implicitly incorporated into social science.

Most practical theology begins with a "thick description" of a situation.[5] Formally, a "thick description" refers to multi-layered ways of thinking about practices, situations, or habits. These ways of thinking about the situation may include a variety of social-scientific and traditional approaches, as the situation gives rise to thought. Informally, people know that any situation in the modern world is multifaceted.[6] The mother who is concerned about her child, for example, implicitly knows that the child's behavior must be considered in relation to several levels of factors interacting together: the child's genetic make-up and personality; the relationships in the family of which the child is a part; the community and institutions, such as the school or church, in which the child participates; social policy which regulates services to the child; and larger cultural beliefs which create an ethos about the child. It is rare that the problem is the result of only one of these factors. As I describe the dynamics of poverty of women and children in the first two chapters, I will include elements of sociological, psychological, economic, and cultural analysis, looking particularly at the way that those kinds of analysis have contributed to public rhetoric about women's poverty.

Practical theology then attempts to uncover the theological assumptions which are implicit in the social scientific analyses. Most social scientists of family policy seem to assume that "self-sufficiency," and its alternatives, are social scientific concepts. Occasionally, social scientists recognize the influence of culture and tradition when they discuss the "values" behind U.S. social policy.[7] Social policy makers rarely recognize the religious roots of these values; in particular, they have never recognized that the debate over self-sufficiency has a long philosophical and theological history which is central to theological tradition.

The historical debate over self-sufficiency is part of the "classic tradition" of theology and is well-recognized by theologians, if not by social scientists. One strand of this tradition, the way that reflection upon the poverty of women and children caused theologians to doubt the notions of self-sufficiency, will be new to most theologians. Luther and Wesley have been chosen as representatives of the theological tradition because their conflicts over the notion of self-sufficiency were guided by their observations of poor women and children in their midst. As a result, they created partial alternatives to the notion of self-sufficiency which can enrich our discussion today.

American thought on self-sufficiency and interdependence is also informed by civic tradition. Americans learn from elementary school on that "classic" American tradition has elevated the values of self-reliance, the self-made "man," and "rugged individualism." Our founding fathers and mothers, however, assumed the importance of interdependence.

24

Thomas Jefferson, who stressed the importance of the individual, walked with a poor woman on the road in France; he, like Luther and Wesley, was drawn by this encounter into reflections upon the responsibilities of society toward the poor. Jefferson's thought had direct bearing on the formal birth of the U.S. woman movement* in 1848 when "The Declaration of Independence" became the prototype for "The Declaration of Sentiments" through which women declared their equal rights with men. In a lesser-known strand of American tradition, the 19th-century woman movement and the 20th-century feminist movement debated the relationship between women's self-sufficiency and women's interdependence. These traditions reveal the source of American women's ambivalence toward the development of a comprehensive family policy.

Finally, practical theology aims to produce recommendations for transformative practice. The dialogue between social scientific approaches to family policy and the theological and civic traditions of self-sufficiency and its alternatives helps to chart the limits and possibilities of family policy as it is developing—or not developing—in the United States today. The seventh chapter will present the theological argument for an articulate family policy, one which can eliminate the poverty of women and children, if Americans will do so.

Ultimately, my point is that "self-sufficiency" is misguided as a norm upon which to base policies concerning single parents and their children. The problem with self-sufficiency as a norm for policy is that it conceals the interconnections between individuals, families, social institutions, and government which are essential for human flourishing. Theologi-

---

*Women have named the movements of which they were a part differently in different historical periods. Activists for women's rights in the 19th century considered themselves part of "the woman movement." The names "feminism" and "the feminist movement" arose in the early 20th century in both Europe and the United States. I will honor the names which these women have themselves given to their movements, using the collective term "women's movement" only when referring to the *entire* public women's tradition.

CHAPTER 1

The Situation of the Female-Headed Household

Poverty . . . is the lack of resources necessary to permit participation in the activities, customs, and diets commonly approved by society.

Peter Townsend[1]

As I made my final preparations to lead worship one Sunday morning in 1982, I opened the church bulletin and found an insert headlined: *Single-Parent Families: A Seed-Bed For Trouble.* The insert asked the congregation to contribute to a special offering for a denominational agency which was well-respected for its work in extremely poor, largely black, areas of the city. I supported the agency's work, but the headline jarred me. I, and the other single parents in my congregation, were raising delightful and well-adjusted children. We faced a variety of difficulties, some of which were shared by nuclear families in the congregation but many of which were not. Similarly, I believed that many poor, black single parents, whose resources might be quite different from my own, had goals similar to mine.

If I drew attention to the insert during the offering, I would be singling out all of these single parents and their children, proclaiming that our families were dangerous. Most disturbing, I knew I would be conjuring up stereotypes of the black poor as irresponsible, promiscuous, and violent in the minds of many of my white, suburban congregants. Many of the congregants would give, and give generously, grateful for their distance from the danger. Some would give, and give humbly, understanding in their hearts what I said when I introduced the insert:

> I read this morning's bulletin insert with ambivalence. As a single parent, I am trying to provide the best care possible for my children, and I do not believe that the single-parent family is a seed-bed for trouble. My children are happy and well-adjusted, not only because of my efforts, but because members of this congregation, acting upon the vows they make at the baptism of every child, have cared for them in particular and concrete ways. Many parents, in single-parent and nuclear families, do not have the benefit of such care. I ask you to give, not because single-parent families are a seed-bed for trouble, but because families beyond the immediate visibility of this congregation deserve our support.

The conflict I faced in this incident is a reminder of long-standing American ambivalence toward the single-parent, mother-headed family.* Historians generally agree that Americans of the colonial and constitutional eras had a generous spirit toward the poor in their midst, believing that the immediate family and the community should help in times of need. Even a historian who is most critical of the social welfare history of the United States, Mimi Abramovitz, acknowledges that "the earliest colonial leaders accepted both the presence of poverty and the obligation of the family and the community to aid the poor. In contrast to later times, the need for relief did not necessarily suggest personal failure or create suspi-

*Much writing and many statistical categories obscure the visibility of fathers and mothers who are single parents. Single-parent families are largely female-headed although increasing numbers of single fathers are heavily involved in child-raising. Frequently, households called "male-headed" are in reality couple-headed households. "Single-parent" households are assumed to be "female-headed," and multigenerational households, headed by grandmothers, mothers, and their children are mixed with single-parent, female-headed households. For precision, I will refer to mother-, father-, or couple-headed families, or female-, male-, or couple-headed households, except when I am quoting another source which uses alternate terms, such as "single parent."

cion."[2] Even so, people in constitutional America nuanced their attitudes toward poor single mothers and their children. If a woman was seen as having created her fate, she and her children were "undeserving"; if she was a victim of circumstance, they were "deserving." This practical rule of thumb, however, easily broke down. Widows and orphans who had not established residence in a particular community were shifted from jurisdiction to jurisdiction. Even a married woman with an established residence had few economic rights of her own. If her husband died a debtor, her dowry might be claimed to pay creditors, leaving her without assets, skills, or property. If a husband had Tory sympathies, some states required that a woman declare a separate political allegiance in order to retain the family property; others expected her to abandon her property to join her husband.[3] The general attitude of early American generosity toward the poor was nuanced with suspicion of single mothers and their children.

Since colonial and constitutional times, Americans' attitudes of generosity and suspicion have informed their struggle with questions such as: Who is responsible for the support of single mothers and their children? Should individual parents, regardless of their circumstances, be held responsible for the care of the children they create? Should the extended family care for these families? What are the obligations of the community, the church, or the government toward the care of single mothers and their children?

Today, the answer to these questions must take into account a cultural, social, and economic situation which is very different from the one of colonial and constitutional times. Women have claimed equal rights with men as citizens—civic rights include not only the right to vote but the right to get a job. Some women have risen through the ranks of upper echelon careers, giving the appearance that all women are economically more secure. Others, however, work at ever-increasing numbers of minimum wage, low-benefit jobs generated by advanced capitalism. Family life has changed immensely. Husbands' and wives' present freedom to divorce would have confounded the colonial people. Families have fewer children, and these children are an economic liability rather than an economic asset. Families are expected to move across the country as the job market dictates and rarely develop strong community loyalties. People were thought to have lost interest in religion, but the political and economic clout of the religious right in the 1980s has called that assumption into question. Suspicion of the poor has increased. In the midst of all of these changes, the number of mother-headed families has risen dramatically, recalling us to the same questions which faced the colonial and constitutional people: Why are these families so vulnerable to poverty? How can poverty be eradicated among female-headed households? Who is responsible for their support? What public voices are offering answers to these questions?

Single-Mother Families and Their Vulnerability to Poverty

The spirits of generosity and suspicion toward mother-headed families is evident in the theories which attempt to explain the rise of female-headed households in the United States and their vulnerability to poverty. In the last four decades poor, female-headed households have arisen in significant numbers in all races and socioeconomic groups in the United States. Social scientists have agreed that the female-headed household is the family form most vulnerable to poverty. If we knew what created the trend toward this family type, some policy makers imply, we might be able to reverse the trend and eradicate such widespread poverty among women and children.

Such reasoning, which allows policy makers to simultaneously seem generous toward children and be suspicious of their mothers, is faulty. A decrease in the number of female-headed households would not reduce their vulnerability to poverty; it would only reduce their visibility and their access to political and social attention. Furthermore, when theories about the emergence of the female-headed household are confused with theories about the poverty of this family form, they tend to perpetuate misconceptions about gender, race and class. Rather than asking what creates the female-headed household, a question born of suspicion, we need to ask, "What creates the *poverty* of the female-headed household?" The following popularly-held theories and explanations are misleading for two reasons: first, they attempt to explain the rise in female-headed households, as if that could account for its poverty; and second, they tend to perpetuate misguided stereotypes about gender, race, and/or class.

1. *The rise of female-headed families is the result of the breakdown of the nuclear family.* This statement is true, almost by definition; however, the terms of the statement are based on assumptions which perpetuate suspicion of the female-headed household. First, the nuclear family, which is assumed to be a father-breadwinner, a mother-homemaker, and at least two children, symbolizes a golden age of family bliss. Second, this nuclear family is also considered the norm for family life. Therefore, the female-headed household, regardless of its problems, its possibilities, its efforts, or its effects, is considered subversive of the nuclear family. The poverty of the female-headed household only seems to confirm its tendency to undermine all family life. In an effort to support one kind of family life, some people uncritically link the development of the family form to explanations of the poverty of the family form.

This line of thinking ignores the history of family change. Through the course of history, the family has included many different people, served many different economic, social, and psychological functions, and has served different purposes in relation to other social groups. For most of history the family has included an extended network of kin. The nuclear family, a relatively new family form which began to emerge under European capitalism, became the dominant family form in the United States under the influence of American mobility patterns of the last two centuries.

The rise of the nuclear family ideal represented changes in the extended family system. The extended family ideal, in which grandparents, aunts, uncles, and cousins lived within proximity to one another and were available to one another for practical help and entertainment, predominated during early European capitalism. It still exists in various forms in most of the world, including in Europe. The extended family provided a wide variety of adults who shared practical tasks, who socialized children into norms and values of the community and taught them skills for living, who provided a selection of role models and confidantes for children, and who represented a safety net of material and economic resources for one another. The extended family tended to constrain the individuality of a particular member, but it provided dependable support for its members.[4]

The actual patterns of work and domesticity of nuclear families, as a unit of two parents and children, are not as homogeneous as popularly believed. The nuclear family unit of two parents and children developed as economic necessity, and cultural ideals, such as glorification of the "self-made man," required that families and family members become more mobile. Middle-class families, who could afford to support the unemployed homemaker-mother, were free to move from area to area; working-class families, in which both spouses were employed, often developed patterns of male-mobility and absence. In almost all but agricultural families, employment outside the home and domesticity within the home developed. Likewise, the middle-class norm which assigned responsibilities for employment and domesticity to men and women, respectively, became the cultural ideal, even when men and women did not exclusively fulfill these roles, as in many white working-class and black families. If one considers a cross-section of American life, the "normative nuclear family" had many variations.

Furthermore, the ideal of the blissful nuclear family ignores both the extent to which intergenerational support contributed to its bliss and the difficulties the nuclear family encountered when it was cut off from that support. Those who idealize the nuclear family forget that more than two adults are needed to raise a child. The nuclear families of

Americans' dreams have received support from a variety of informal family and community sources. Inevitably, nuclear families whose extended families have broken down must find other adults who function as grandparents, aunts, uncles and cousins; frequently, however, these adults do not have an unconditional emotional or economic commitment to the multiple generations. When a nuclear family cannot depend on the wider support of the extended family, and in addition, one parent spends most of his or her time away from home making money, and the other remains within the home providing all domestic care, the phenomena of distant fathering, overinvolved mothering, and physical and economic strain develop.

When a female-headed household arises within a well-connected extended family, the family often can absorb the female-headed household in such a way as to substantially reduce the extent to which that household will be impoverished economically, materially, or emotionally. This kind of extended family support has been an important factor in poor black families' survival and resilience. Evidence is developing, however, which suggests that the extended family support networks among black families are also breaking down. When a female-headed household arises from a middle-class nuclear household, the female-headed household frequently flounders without economic, material, or emotional support. If we consider these dynamics, the female-headed household exists within a larger family and community system. It cannot be expected to be economically, psychologically, and socially self-sufficient; the unrealistic ideals and expectations against which it is measured contribute to its poverty.

2. *The rise in black female-headed families can be attributed to a "culture of poverty."* The concept of a culture of poverty originally helped to explain how people in non-western cultures were able to survive as they adapted to poverty-stricken conditions. As it has been used to explain American poverty, however, the idea has been widely criticized for the portion of its thesis which concludes that a culture of poverty among blacks, dating back to slavery, created pathological

character traits in individuals who passed them to succeeding generations. Specifically, the concept of a *black culture of poverty* perpetuates the belief that all black families have a long history of female-headedness and instability; that this history has created individual, psychological traits which perpetuate poverty; and that these traits are handed down through the generations, socializing young blacks into poverty. Such reasoning creates the impression that most of the black population will inevitably be poor.

Most of these conclusions have been disproved by recent research. For example, William Julius Wilson's *The Truly Disadvantaged: The Inner City, the Underclass, and Public Policy* shows that in contrast to the popular image of black family instability, most lower-class black families were intact through the Second World War.[5] Prior to that time, if female-headed families arose among blacks, a parent had usually died or was absent in search of employment. From the time of World War II, however, widowhood declined as a cause of single-parent families and divorce and separation became more frequent. In the period from 1940 to 1960, the divorce and separation rate rose among blacks from 29.1% to 71.3% and among whites from 27.2% to 36.8%.[6] Divorce and separation became more common among all groups but increased most among lower-class blacks. When we talk of the rise of female-headed households in the U.S., therefore, we must date the beginning of that rise to the late 1940s, not the early 1970s. Most recently, the rise of never-married mothers has increased the predominance of female-headed households among lower-class blacks. Both non-marital pregnancy and premarital pregnancy has increased, in Wilson's words, into "an unprecedented rate of out-of-wedlock births." Furthermore, married women bear fewer children.

From these data we know that the black nuclear family was relatively stable for at least eighty years after the end of slavery. The female-headed households in the lower-class black population took different forms in different generations, resulting first from widowhood, then from separation or divorce, and most recently from out-of-wedlock pregnancy.

Thus we cannot attribute the poverty of the female-headed black family either to a long history of family instability or to intergenerational black psychological traits. Although "culture of poverty" arguments referring to groups in the United States are most frequently associated with the black population, these kinds of arguments are too easily transferable to groups in the U.S. with large concentrations of poverty, such as Latin Americans or Native Americans. These arguments may obscure the particularities of poverty among these groups while ignoring the benefits for all of universalized programs.*

3. *The welfare expansion of the 1960s is responsible for the rise of black, out-of-wedlock births which created the rise in female-headed households.* The idea that welfare creates dependency is used to explain why some women do not seem motivated to find and land jobs which would get them off welfare. Behind this theory is the assumption that poor mothers prefer to get something for nothing, rather than exert themselves a bit more in the workforce in order to raise their standard of living. If they would exert themselves, they wouldn't be poor; since they are poor, they must be lazy, also. This argument is carried more by suspicion of poor mothers than by logic. It fails to take into account that many middle-class mothers also are not employed but are not deemed lazy by society. In fact, workfare proponents argued that one reason to make poor mothers work is that they will work! This argument fails to take account of the effects of programs which target the poor. Invariably, targeted programs create a differential between the income and benefits of welfare (which are below poverty level) and income and benefits from a part-time, minimum wage job (which are below welfare). If a woman can only find a service-sector job, receives no health benefits with her job, and cannot find affordable child care,

*In this work I contrast poverty among black women and white women as a way of making the point that women's poverties in the United States are highly contextual. Rather than speaking of "women's poverty," I follow Michael Harrington's lead preferring to speak of "women's poverties." We need to recognize the particularities of various poverties which develop among different racial, ethnic, and geographical populations.

she may make what under other circumstances would be deemed a smart decision and remain on welfare.

Furthermore, the data presented above dispel the notion that welfare creates dependency among female-headed households. The great rise in female-headed black households occurred before the institution of welfare in the 1960s as a result of separation and divorce; therefore, the popular notion of the black welfare mother who has babies in order to collect more money from the government is an anachronism. If anything, the expansion of welfare correlates to the rise in middle-class and white female-headed households; but most of these female-headed households have resulted from divorce, not from out-of-wedlock pregnancy. Therefore, the 1960s welfare programs cannot even explain the rise in female-headed households, much less account for their poverty.

4. *The lack of employed, marriageable men accounts for the rise of female-headed households in the black underclass.* The correlation between inner city unemployment and black teenage pregnancy has been noted by many researchers. Heather L. Ross and Isabell V. Sawhill of the Urban Institute identified this trend as early as 1975.[7] Most recently, William Julius Wilson has popularized this conclusion with updated data in *The Truly Disadvantaged.* Wilson argues that high rates of unemployment, homicide, and incarceration among young black men in underclass communities so substantially reduce the possibility of young women marrying employed men that female-headed households comprise up to 97% of the families of some communities. Wilson emphasizes that jobs must be created for black men so that they will be in a position to form families.[8]

Wilson provides an important analysis which must be factored into the understanding of black female-headed families' destitution. Underclass men must find good employment opportunities in order for underclass communities to be revitalized, and community stabilization will help underclass women. Since the rate of inadequate support or nonsupport by men is generally high, however, one cannot assume that a higher rate of employment among black males would result directly in eradicating poverty among women and children. Wilson's thesis about the reciprocity between the declining number of marriageable men and the rise of single-parent households does not fully explain why women in these communities are impoverished, nor does his thesis provide support for public policy interventions which would necessarily reduce the poverty of women and children in these communities.

5. *Divorce, particularly no-fault divorce, impoverishes female-headed families.* Divorce correlates with the rise of female-headed households in both the black and the white populations. Divorce has a wide range of economic results for women. Lenore Weitzman has argued that "no-fault divorce" produced wildly variable economic results among female-headed households of all socioeconomic groups. "No-fault" means that blame is not attributed to one divorcing spouse or the other. With the elimination of blame, the idea of financial reward or penalty in divorce is also eliminated. In its place, spouses receive either an "equal" or "equitable" distribution of resources.

Divorce, as a dissolution of the nuclear family, does create female-headed households, but these households need be no more or less poor than the single-parent, male-headed households which are also created by divorce. Many factors help to create situations in which women are impoverished by divorce and men are not. Social-structural factors, such as women's secondary place in the economy; personal factors, such as a women's education and training, whether she maintained a career or expected to be a homemaker, and whether she dropped out of the work force when she bore children; and the equity of divorce agreements—all these work together to create women's economic status after divorce. "No-fault" is not the factor which penalizes women unfairly since, under the fault system, women can be blamed (and therefore, impoverished) as well as men.

As long as we ask the question of what creates the family form, rather than what creates its vulnerability to poverty, female-headed households will remain poor.

Female-Headed Households: Understanding Without Suspicion

What creates the widespread *vulnerability* of the female-headed household to poverty? Although many people can point to examples of women who have risen to the top of the corporate pay scale, of husbands who are left destitute by divorce, and of couples who care jointly and equitably for children, these examples do not represent the norm for women as a group. Female-headed households are vulnerable to poverty due to the sexual and racial divisions of labor which continue to give women a secondary place in the socioeconomic structure of the United States. In addition, due to child custody and support practices, female-headed households usually carry heavier economic and emotional responsibilities for children than do male-headed households but have access to fewer economic resources. Furthermore, women in female-headed households are less able to compete for higher places in the economic structure because their responsibilities for children conflict with their availability for economic competition. Finally, the macroeconomic processes of advanced capitalism have depleted the communities where female-headed households are most concentrated, particularly in the inner city. These conditions point toward three main themes: (1) the economic situation facing all women as women; (2) the economic situation facing women who mother; (3) the economic situation facing black women, which is instructive of, but not identical to, the situation faced by women of other minority groups.

These themes have been discussed in general sociological literature on the changing quality of poverty in the 1970s and 1980s. Some of these studies documented a growing "feminization of poverty," a phrase originated in 1978 by Diana Pearce, a senior research analyst at Catholic University of America. As that term became popularized, it also became vague. Many women, particularly women of color, objected to the misconceptions which were perpetuated when the "feminization of poverty" drew attention to the problems of middle-class women who were divorcing. However, Pearce's two articles, "Is Poverty Being Feminized in America?" and "The Feminization of Ghetto Poverty," taken together, offer a good summary of the themes of many other poverty studies of the 1970s and 1980s.[9] The data gathered under the banner of "the feminization of poverty" is important, although the rhetoric for and against that term can be misleading. As always, the conclusions drawn on the basis of data must be critically scrutinized. I am drawing my summary from sociological (not popular) works, inclusive of, but not restricted to, those which use that phrase. The phrase, in my opinion, has become so vague as to lead to many misconceptions, and theologians should be wary of its use.

The Economic Situation Facing All Women

All women are subject to sexual economic discrimination. This discrimination hits women on a variety of levels: through the sexual "occupational ghetto," through private and public income transfers, and through macroeconomic processes.

Overall, women over the last three decades continue to be paid roughly one-third less in salary, wages, and benefits than men. In contrast to the popular image of the briefcase-carrying woman, most women have not embarked on well-paid careers; rather, they engage in temporary, low-paid, part-time employment. Part-time jobs rarely make a woman eligible for insurance and pension benefits. She is not eligible for social security programs, such as unemployment insurance, which are built on the assumption of full-time work. A woman engaging in part-time work is frequently seen by employers as less committed and more dispensable than the full time worker. She is assumed to be earning "extra" money for the household.

Barbara Ehrenreich and Frances Fox Piven have pointed out that this situation is exacerbated by the public policy assumption that men should earn a "family wage"—the salary and benefits package which enables men to provide for a family. The gain of a family wage for the working class men was a prime achievement of union organizers of the 1930s; but many men, including a large portion of black men, never earned a family wage. For many women whose primary responsibility was domestic homemaking, the system of low-paid, "extra" jobs for women seemed to work well in the context of a male breadwinner's family wage. This system masked the potential poverty of women whose households no longer contained a male breadwinner.[10]

These assumptions about women's secondary economic role within the family interact with contemporary macroeconomic trends, creating a further entrenchment of women's "occupational ghetto." As the manufacturing of goods gives way to service-oriented industries, jobs which are inadequate as an economic base for raising a family multiply. Women are employed in 70% of these jobs.[11] Likewise, automation reduces the need for skilled employment, replacing it with low-paid, unskilled jobs. Many of these jobs become "women's work" although, as we will note later, the employment of poor and minority men and youth is similarly influenced by the same macroeconomic processes. Furthermore, the cost of housing has skyrocketed in the last two decades, and this cost cannot be absorbed into the budget of a family dependent upon menial work for its livelihood.

The Economic Situation Facing Mothers

The economic situation for women further breaks down when the difficulties which women face in the workplace are compounded by motherhood. Although the public image of the working woman from the 1970s was one in which women avoided or postponed childbirth, as Ruth Sidel points out in *Women and Children Last*, "most women become mothers."[12] Even though women have increasingly worked outside the home, in both marriage and divorce they have continued to bear primary household and child care responsibilities. Teenage mothers who have not completed their education are especially vulnerable to long-term poverty. When women raise children alone, the amount of money women need in

40

order to support their families increases. Women's access to the work force, however, frequently decreases. Women's place in the public support system may change, depending upon their circumstances.[13]

Unless women are career-oriented, they will not easily earn enough money to support children. Women across the socioeconomic spectrum may not prepare themselves for earning a family wage for a number of reasons.[14] Traditionally, women have not been socialized toward family breadwinning, so neither their families nor their communities have expected a women to prepare for earning a family wage. Young women themselves may not see the need to prepare themselves for family breadwinning. Because of these cultural assumptions, women as a group have been less likely than men to receive intergenerational transfers of resources, such as a family investment in their education.

These cultural expectations may be changing. Changes in welfare policy, which *require* that mothers with children ages three and older be in job training or be working at paid work, and pressure in divorce courts to expect all divorcing women to be employed, indicate new social expectations of women. In a new study of young women, ages 12–25, Ruth Sidel discovered that most young women themselves expect to combine family with some form of paid work. While cultural assumptions are changing, Sidel found that young women from all social backgrounds are unrealistic about the difficulties of supporting a family as a mother.[15] In today's public and private domestic policy climate, single mothers and their children are only financially secure when mothers earn enough money not only to support themselves but also to support a family.

Divorce and separation have historically created a dramatic situation in which women and children have lost economic security.[16] Public policy and public traditions have diverged over the purpose of the family wage. Although public policy supported the concept of the family wage based on the assumption that a man should support a wife and children, this assumption did not extend to a man who was separated from his family through divorce. In the case of divorce, social convention adhered to the belief that the money he earned was "his money." Until very recently, social convention has not expected men to pay child support payments. Although women have been awarded alimony and child support payments by the courts, individual women have had to initiate the process of support enforcement, weighing the value of collecting the award against the emotional and financial costs of a court battle. Since they have not been able to rely on the courts and government to enforce their own judgments, billions of support payments remain unpaid each year. Even though the present domestic legal and cultural climate has moved toward enforcing the payment of child support, particularly when non-support forces a woman onto welfare, legal child support awards are often inadequate. Furthermore, in the climate of an expectation of women's work, many states have dropped the concept of alimony or maintenance, except for very limited time periods. The courts expect that divorced and separated women will engage in paid work.

The support of children creates counterforces in women's relationship to the work force. Women are pulled toward the work force by the need for additional income in order to support children, but they are pulled away from the work force by their primary responsibilities for child care. All women who mother must either care for their children themselves, gain help from family and friends, or pay the high costs of child care. The cost of reliable, licensed child care easily absorbs a large portion of the wages of a woman who is earning a family wage or less. When children are sick and working women must be absent from their jobs, women are often seen as "less dependable" or "less committed" employees. When women have become pregnant, there have been few workplace structures which offer a woman enough time off for childbirth and recuperation and then allow her to return to her job. Some corporations are beginning to change their benefits to accommodate a female work force, but these benefits will reach the most privileged of employed women first, having little immediate benefit for those who are poor. The combination of these circumstances frequently creates the need for female-headed households to rely on public economic transfers. Just as there is a dual labor market in which the primary market receives family wages and benefits and the secondary market receives secondary wages, there is a dual market in public transfers.[17] The primary market, which offers the most substantial benefits, includes military benefits, social security, and unemployment and survivors' insurance. The primary market is aimed at eliminating poverty among certain groups of people: veterans, the elderly, the widowed, and those who are temporarily unemployed from full time employment. The secondary market contains substantially reduced benefits for women and children. It is designed not to compete with low-wage jobs which attract women employees, nor is it supposed to eliminate poverty. The most consistent program of this kind is Aid to Families with Dependent Children (AFDC), although various workfare programs fall into this category.

Aid to Dependent Children (ADC), the predecessor to AFDC, was popularly understood to be a program which allowed poor children to remain in the home with their mothers, an alternative to placing them in orphanages. This motive is called into question, however, by the fact that welfare benefits have traditionally been set low enough not to compete with low wage work. AFDC has never provided a family wage, and supplementary earnings which would bring female-headed households to family wage levels make a female-headed household ineligible for AFDC.[18] This circumstance has forced many AFDC mothers to participate in the irregular economy of unreported income, such as domestic employment as maids, babysitters, etc.

Under the Reagan administration AFDC eligibility was further restricted. The cutback hurts women in at least two ways. Obviously, a smaller portion of impoverished female-headed families are receiving AFDC benefits, although the number of those families have grown so tremendously that more such families receive AFDC than ever before. Furthermore, the welfare system employs primarily women.[19] As welfare programs are cut, so are the jobs available to women. Sidel and Piven note that it is not unusual for women to go from distributing welfare to receiving welfare. The Bush administration has continued to apply pressure to reduce welfare spending.

The Special Problems of Black Women

In her 1983 article, Pearce argues that black mothers face both gender and race discrimination. Many black women are especially vulnerable to poverty due to the structurally reinforced economic vulnerability of the black community. They are frequently forced into the secondary labor market as well as the secondary welfare system. Poor black women are more likely to create female-headed households due to the high rates of out-of-wedlock pregnancy, separation, and divorce in the inner-city community. Many black women are separated without having a legal agreement or court-ordered support rights; they are also less likely to remarry than whites. As a result, when we ask whether a woman is more likely to be poor if she is a black woman or a white woman, race is more significant than gender: the percentage of poor black female-headed families in the total black population is substantially higher than the percentage of whites. If we ask whether, in the total population, the poor households are more likely to be female-headed or black, gender is more important than race: the actual number of poor white female-headed households is higher than the actual number of poor black households.

Women of color who criticized the concept of "the feminization of poverty" contended that it ignored the poverty of black men. Pearce, anticipating the thesis that William Julius Wilson would popularize through *The Truly Disadvantaged,* noted that the rate of female-headedness in black families was related to the decreased number of marriageable men in black inner-city communities.[20] Because of the combination of the present low marriage rate and the structurally-created discrimination against black women, black women in inner-city communities carried the triple economic burden of being black, being female, and living in an underclass community. Pearce also noted that couple-headed black households were more likely to be the recipients of socioeconomic advances for blacks than female-headed black households. The black community, she claimed, was polarizing along the lines of marital status.[21]

Who Has the Answers?
Resolving Our Ambivalence About Mothers

American ambivalence toward single mothers and their children, which arises from our conflicting beliefs about them, the family, and society, greatly influences our interpretation of the data before us. Several groups of thinkers, in proposing solutions to the poverty of female-headed families, have used the language of self-sufficiency in order to resolve this ambivalence. In their policy positions these groups emphasize, variously, the responsibilities of the individual woman, the family, and the federal government. Each has a particular perspective on the role of self-sufficiency in eliminating women's poverties.

First, true believers in personal self-sufficiency continue to think that welfare creates a free ride for poor mothers. The problem of poverty in the female-headed family can be attributed largely to the absence of the work ethic among these women. The answer to all poverty, in their view, is increased economic opportunity. They applaud the welfare reform of 1988 in which mothers are expected to be employed if their children are aged three or older. Only in the most extreme circumstances should a mother be supported by public means, and only if she can show herself to be "deserving" of this help.

Second, advocates of divorce law reform concentrate largely on the relationship between women's poverties and nuclear family breakdown. They have identified the problem as residing within the distribution of goods and services in the family after divorce and separation. Lenore Weitzman, who wrote *The Divorce Revolution*, is noted for her exposure of inadequately awarded and collected child support settlements, of the way that changes in the divorce law have dramatically different results for women of different ages groups, and of the economic inequities that result from women's different place in the socioeconomic structure. Other commentators on divorce law reform suggest that the inequities of divorce will cease to exist if mothers and fathers are held equally responsible for the economic support and day-to-day care of their children. Despite their different suggestions about the best route to equity, these commentators have in common the fundamental conviction that the support of female-headed households can best be assured through equity in family law. The goal of mothers' "self-sufficiency," in the terms of this discussion, depends upon providing a divorced, separated, or unwed mother with enough of the family's resources to enable her to become economically competitive.

Third, advocates of universalized family policies argue that mother-headed families will be vulnerable to poverty until federal legislation provides for basic, minimal care for all persons. This group speaks of self-sufficiency as enabled by a public "safety net" which insures families' basic needs. They point out that the United States has a high rate of poverty among women and children in contrast to other industrialized countries, such as Austria, Denmark, West Germany, France, Israel, Sweden, the Netherlands. In these seven countries the support of female-headed households is believed to be a *public*, not only a private family, responsibility. A public authority, first, guarantees child support by advancing support payments to the caretaking parent; and second, assumes the responsibility for collecting child support from the absent parent.[22] In addition, these countries have family policies which support women's abilities to bear children and work in the workplace, such as extended maternity leave and job protection, child care, and socialized health care. These commentators argue that such "dependencies" on government are not more harmful than the kind of dependencies people with resources develop within the family or the local community. These countries have a lower standard of living than the U.S., but they also have low rates of poverty among women and children and do not speak of a developing "permanent underclass."

Finally, some commentators argue that larger socioeconomic processes are determining the nature of poverty in the United States. These processes are breaking down communities and isolating the poor from job networks and institutions of social support. These commentators argue that macroeconomic policies provide the context within which family policy and/or individual self-sufficiency projects must be designed.

Commentators on the poverty of the female-headed household rarely constitute a "pure type," arguing for only one solution and eschewing all others. They do emphasize one solution over others, however, and the definition of self-sufficiency changes when the primary solution changes. In reflecting on solutions to the problem of women's and children's poverty, we will consider the best data we have at hand and whether it seems to make sense. As we interpret the data, we will inevitably ask ourselves, How does the data interact with what we believe? How do we enter into public discourse about what we believe? In this case, what do we believe about the self-sufficiency of single mothers and their children, the family, and the society in which they live? If we understand our cultural, political, and religious beliefs about self-sufficiency, we will be in a better position to assess the rhetoric on behalf of the various solutions.

CHAPTER 2

The Rhetoric of Equality

We are exporting a casual acceptance of—even a commitment to—human deprivation, to unemployment, inflation,
and disastrously reduced living standards. This is even seen
as essential therapy: out of the experience of unemployment and hunger will come a new and revitalized work
ethic, a working force eager for the discipline of free enter-
prise. . . . In one ardently expressed view, which I heard just
a few days ago from a business adviser recently returned
from Poland, such deprivation—unemployment, low
wages—will cause foreign investors and entrepreneurs in
years ahead to come in for the rescue. Only a few years of
suffering and all will be well. This, I choose my words
carefully, is insanity.

John Kenneth Galbraith[1]

In the last three decades the fight for equal rights for
women has increased women's access to many male-dominated roles in society, including in the church and the academy. As women have worked in those roles, they have
discovered that the traditional rules of the workplace (including the rules under which churchwomen were educated and
employed) did not easily accommodate their permanent presence. American beliefs about gender, about what women and
men can and should do, seem to have changed, but the rules
under which men and women are employed remain largely
the same. The traditional rules of the workplace are, first, that
a man (or woman employed in a male role) must marshall his

full resources in the service of competing in the workplace, and second, that he must make his family provide support for his career, or at the very least, that he must not allow duties to family, other than breadwinning, to interfere with his employment.

These rules have guided theological education and the church, as well as secular employment: for example, those students who have adequate financial and personal support to follow the usual full-time track will usually compete better than those with heavy financial and caring obligations; and pastors must follow these rules and learn to couch them in theological language in order to compete in most church polity systems.

Women's lives do not easily accommodate these rules. When I make a mental survey of the women I have known in seminaries, churches, and pastoral care agencies, I find that they have coped with these rules in four basic ways. Each coping style leads to an experience of women's work which encourages a different normative understanding of equality.

1. *Some women become "competitors."* Competitors frequently do not marry and/or mother, preferring to free themselves to compete in the secular, academic or ecclesial market under traditional conditions. They have risen to the challenge of proving that women can compete in traditionally male workworlds, and they frequently are the first to break into influential public roles. Their female colleagues often criticize them as "climbing the male ladder," and competitors are often unsympathetic toward women who do not make similar choices. Implicit in competitors' choices is an understanding of equality as equal access for women to the male workworld of economic success, status, power, and influence.

2. *Some women become "innovators."* Innovators integrate family and employment by creating alternative life routes which reduce the pressure created by family and work. These women often find a personally satisfying and compatible integration of roles, and their path is often idealized by church women as "breaking the male mold," but they rarely attain the public influence of the competitor. Some men

respond to innovators by either not taking them seriously, by being frustrated at their attempts to reorganize the rules, or by being pleased when they find their own way. Implicit in innovators' choices is women's equal right to self-determination. Self-determination requires that a woman be able to "work around the system," reorganizing the resources of the workplace and family to enhance her personal options and her environmental flexibility in determining the relationship between employment and family in her individual life.

3. *Some women become "heroines."* These women are married and/or mother and, as "superwomen," compete successfully in traditional conditions. Heroines are well-liked by male colleagues because they usually work within the rules, but they also provide role modeling for men who want to integrate their lifestyles. They are often isolated from female colleagues because of intense work/family demands, or because they follow too many traditionally-female rules for the competitors and too many traditionally-male rules for the innovators. If working in traditional conditions creates severe consequences for their families and themselves, they occasionally become competitors or innovators, frequently suffer quietly in an extremely stressful balancing act, and more and more frequently, drop out at mid-career. Heroines challenge the belief that men may have fulfilling employment and a family while women must choose employment or family. Heroines' implicit commitment to equality suggests that women's and men's equality is dependent upon each gender's sharing economic and domestic responsibilities.

4. *Some women become "survivors."* Survivors are frequently employed in traditionally female jobs which have always provided necessary services without which the workplace could not function. Service providers often seek the reduced responsibility of traditionally female jobs in the hope that they can prioritize their responsibilities on the homefront. They pay a heavy price for this trade-off. They frequently discover that they are expected to take on more responsibility than their title would signify, while others get the credit, and they receive the wages and benefits which do not qualify as a

family wage. Male and female colleagues often consider these women expendable, an extension of technology rather than a contributing member of the community. Implicit in survivors' hope for equality is economic and relational equity, a family-supporting wage and benefits and respect in return for a job well done.

By choice or by coercion, women are following these diverse paths in the hope that they will contribute to women's equality.[2] How has the rhetoric of equality provided a context for the practices of U.S. policy, and how have these practices, in turn, contributed to women's poverties?

The Rhetoric of Equality

The American belief in equality takes on a rhetoric which responds to an era's cultural concerns and commitments. By "rhetoric" I do not mean "verbal manipulation" as the word is frequently used. Rather, rhetoric, in its classic sense, meant ways of communicating the message, not on the speaker's terms, but in a language common to the speaker and the audience so that the audience could understand. When I use the word "rhetoric," I mean ways of speaking about belief which become persuasive because they have been constructed within the cultural ethos of a time. The rhetoric of equality has constructed the meaning of equality for that time which, in turn, has helped to shape social change. The most recent form of the rhetoric of equality enabled more blacks and women than ever before to enter public life. This language failed many women and blacks, however, because it produced an appearance of equality without addressing the historic sexism, racism, and classism which lay beneath the facade. This appearance of equality was particularly toxic to the female-headed household.

The belief in their right to equality, shared by black people and women, has called on a common language since the beginnings of the abolitionist and woman movements.[3] In the 19th century both blacks and women believed that they had "natural rights" as full persons. Their claim was rooted in religious, political, and familial images. The Americans who supported the Declaration of Independence and the Constitution believed in the "natural" worth of the individual. This religious belief supported the political belief in the natural rights of "man" in society and family, giving rise to American democracy. Women and blacks appealed to these same democratic principles when they claimed that they had natural, inalienable rights. Both groups declared that they, too, were covered by the principle of equal rights which inspired the Declaration of Independence and the U.S. Constitution. The laws of the land, therefore, should recognize their exercise of these rights.

Despite their common language, participants in the abolitionist and woman movements soon discovered that women and blacks faced different kinds of obstacles to their claim on these rights. White men who fought for abolition were not necessarily willing to support the woman movement, and some women could not simultaneously support their own cause and the cause of blacks. Furthermore, the needs and desires of blacks and women were different in the quest for equality. Women of the 19th century recognized a need for a wide range of supports for family life; black men concentrated on gaining the freedom of access to the civic, political, and cultural privileges which were available to white society. This tradition of different quests under a similar rhetoric of equality continued into the civil rights and feminist movements of the late 1950s and early 1960s.

The claims for equality of the feminist and civil rights movements which helped to form social policy in the 1960s were shaped by the ethos of individualism which developed after World War II. The early part of the century had been dominated by a belief in the progress of individuals within social institutions, but the World Wars nearly destroyed that faith in society. Americans looked to the individual as the last great hope for social redemption. American mainline religion, particularly the newly emerging movement of pastoral care and counseling, responded to this new cultural faith in individualism and explored it in depth.[4]

The growing consensus over individualism provided a foundation for attacking social traditions and institutions which had tenaciously held women and blacks "in their place." Spokespersons for the 1960s civil rights and feminist movements necessarily constructed many of their arguments for equality within this consensus. This version of equal rights meant that all individuals, regardless of race or gender, should have the opportunity to compete for society's opportunities. Therefore, individual blacks, women, and children should have equal access to these opportunities. Equal access was impeded by the unequal treatment of individuals; therefore, society was responsible for insuring equal access and treatment of individuals. The civil rights legislation of the 1960s, which fulfilled this expectation, was shaped by this unique language of equality, the rhetoric of "equal opportunity."

Post-World War II individualism formed not only America's political expression of equality in rights, access, opportunity, and treatment, but it also formed America's understanding of equality in relation to personal human fulfillment. The authors of *Habits of the Heart* have identified this ethos of fulfillment as "expressive individualism."[5] Expressive individualism combined personal freedom with the post-War understanding of equality. Equality, in expressive individualism, was built on valuing of each individual's experience, providing equal access of each individual to an intimate relationship, and guaranteeing choice for or against a relationship through equal rights and treatment within the relationship. The American cultural commitment to equal opportunity, therefore, provided the rhetoric for both our political and personal agendas.

Just as the early political movement for natural rights was supported by colonial religion, the equal opportunity agendas were carried on in American mainline religion. The political agenda was continued by religious social activists who made explicit the religious motivations for the civil rights and feminist movements. Institutional sexism and racism in the church were most frequently analyzed primarily in terms of rights, access, opportunity, and treatment. The personal agenda was carried on by the pastoral care movement whose expressivist language grew under the influence of the experiential psychologist, Carl Rogers. Both movements had their roots in the post-War skepticism of institutions and traditions, and both offered religious motivations and practices which promoted the new definition of equality.

This political, personal, and religious agenda revolved around an optimistic attitude toward the individual. If individuals could overthrow the economic, social and personal structures of domination, they would become free to "maximize their own potential." Among some feminists, "self-sufficiency" could disentangle a woman from the structures of domination and provide her with freedom. Self-sufficiency in the feminist movement referred to the right of the individual to control her economic, emotional, and decision-making life. This optimism was also apparent in attitudes toward the black family and toward divorce.[6] For example, when Daniel Patrick Moynihan wrote a pessimistic prognosis for the black family in his report on *The Negro Family*, in which he first called attention to the growing number of female-headed households, his report was widely criticized.[7] These households were not deviant, his critics charged; they were adaptive. Similarly, when divorce became increasingly widespread, it was no longer considered a failure but an "opportunity for personal growth." This optimism was evident in religious liturgy which, for a period of time, eliminated prayers of confession or relegated them to a perfunctory role.

Optimism and Economics

American optimism about the individual and confidence in this particular form of equality matured in the 1950s and thrived in the 1960s in a period of economic prosperity. The United States and most of its middle-class citizens could literally, economically, *afford* this philosophy. Policy makers anticipated continued economic growth, as when, in 1969 Moynihan wrote that "one of the challenges to government in the future was to devise ways of spending the enormous tax revenues yielded by an everexpanding GNP."[8] Had Moynihan's prediction been accurate, the transition from civil to economic equality for blacks and women might have materialized.

Leaders such as Martin Luther King knew that equal opportunity was essential but that it could not substitute for economic equality. People who studied poverty, such as Michael Harrington, argued that equal opportunity would not produce economic equality, or "equality of outcomes," as it was called. In 1965 President Johnson had begun to recognize the distinctions between the freedom to exercise equal opportunity and equality of outcomes:

> Freedom is not enough. You do not wipe away the scars of centuries by saying: Now you are free to go where you want, do as you desire, choose leaders you please.
>
> You do not take a person who for years has been hobbled by chains and liberate him, bring him up to the starting line of a race and then say, "You are free to compete with all the others," and still justly believe that you have been completely fair. . . . This is the next and more profound stage of the battle for civil rights. We seek not just freedom but opportunity—not just legal equity but human ability—not just equality as a right and a theory, but equality as a fact and as a result.[9]

Even though the President began to move the language of equality in a new direction, the arguments needed to influence policy makers ran against the cultural and economic currents of the day. Culturally, a shift in the rhetoric of equality from equal opportunity for the individual to an equality of outcomes required that optimistic belief in the potential of the individual would need to give way to a realism about the problems of the individual in changing the social situation. In order for policy makers to be able to argue for the importance of an equality of outcomes, the culture had to be prepared to hear that the corruption in the social situation could not be changed by the individual alone.

The optimistic belief in individualism had arisen, however, as a therapy for the disillusionment with the social situation, so a call for attention to the socioeconomic situation was unwelcome.[10] When Moynihan pointed to problems in the inner city, his argument clashed with equal rights rhetoric which was built on the equal capacities of all people to exercise citizenship.[11] If all people could exercise citizenship, they could compete equally. Finally, declining national economics squelched the discussion of what seemed like an even costlier equality of outcomes. The costs of the Vietnam War and the economic roller coaster of the 1970s destroyed the optimism that "economic growth and civil rights could coexist."[12]

Divorce reform legislation was drafted and enacted in the late 1960s and early 1970s in an economically prosperous state, California, during the decline of the national discussion of equality of outcomes. The rhetoric of equal rights, access, treatment, and opportunity, rather than equality of outcomes, in a mixture of its political and personal forms, became the basis for the direction of this reform. The law reflected the trend toward interpreting equality as "equal right to competition" to the extent that it emphasized a strict equality in the division of assets without considering the life conditions of the various members of the family.

Furthermore, divorce law reform developed in the midst of women's changing place in the economic structure after World War II, a place that was particularly precarious. War swings women like a pendulum within the economic structure. During a war women move into traditionally male employment due to the scarcity of male workers, but after a war women resume domestic, unpaid roles. After World War II, women's return to domesticity took a unique form. Sylvia Hewlett notes the paradoxical double ideal which developed: the ideal of ultradomesticity, on one hand, and the ideal of equal civil rights for women, on the other.[13] Women's post-War return to domesticity reflected the reenforcement of patriarchy through public policy and legal incentives; it also reflected a psychological need for families and the culture in general to withdraw to a comfortable hearth and collect its emotional energy after the trauma of war. In post-War prosperity, we could afford domesticity. When a substantial number of women reentered the economic market, the revenues of women as a group and the national GNP rose: it seemed to many that the nation which could afford ultradomesticity could also afford women's individual civil rights.

In the early 1970s a number of trends coincided: a rhetoric of equal rights, access, treatment, and opportunity; a belief that women and blacks were advancing in the economic marketplace; an unpredictable but ultimately declining economy; and divorce reform legislation which was written in one of the more prosperous states. The increase in female-headed households had been noticed, but was generally unacknowledged, in the black population. Now, the divorce rate soared, increasing the female-headed households in the middle-class, largely white population. These households were particularly vulnerable to the racially and sexually discriminatory structure which lay just beneath the facade of civil rights—the facade which began to crumble in the polarization of the economy in the 1980s.[14]

How are we to evaluate the rhetoric of equal rights, access, treatment, and opportunity? Should we, as is becoming fashionable, accuse the feminist movement—and its rhetoric of equality—of being shortsighted? Some women, having reaped the benefits of the feminist movement in terms of public and economic position, have now become critical of its rhetoric of equality. In contrast, I suggest that the rhetoric of equality as it was adopted by both the feminist and civil rights movements was brilliant, necessary, and tragic.

The brilliance of the rhetoric of equality lay in its capacity to develop a message of social change which could ride on the crest of the wave of the gathering momentum of the culture of individualism of the 1950s and 1960s. By developing a message which could make use of the momentum, it converted a time which could have relaxed into economic and psychological ease and gave it a vision which tapped but redirected its conservative tendencies.

The necessity of the rhetoric of equality, sadly, lay in the reality of patriarchy, which continues to dominate the process of social, cultural, and economic advancement for women of any color.* Under patriarchy, the social advancement of women requires that at various times and stages of the process, some women must prove that they can compete as if they were men. To those women who rose to the challenge of competing in a man's "equal rights, access, treatment, and opportunity" world, often giving up what had traditionally been the joys and benefits of a woman's world and experiencing immense conflict and regret in that choice, the rest of us must extend our thanks, rather than only our criticism. Furthermore, the rhetoric of equal opportunity is not dead. It still protects the rights for which women from the 19th century to the 1970s fought, and it is still a necessary rhetoric in some parts of the nation in which women are just beginning to emerge into the public arena.

Its tragedy, however, was its contribution to the poverty of the female-headed household. Tragedy occurs when, despite our best efforts, we fail. The rhetoric of equal opportunity failed to the extent that it could not address the historic racism, sexism or classism which binds our socioeconomic system, nor could it protect from poverty our children or the people who took the primary responsibility for parenting them, overwhelmingly mothers.

The Rhetoric of Equality and the Poverty of Mothers

The rhetoric of equal rights, access, opportunity and treatment shaped the most significant anti-discrimination legislation ever: affirmative action. Several commentators have asked, "why, in the era of the greatest anti-discrimination legislation ever, has the economic situation of women and minorities not improved?" Affirmative action assumes that when the conditions of competition are equal, people can compete equally. Blacks cannot compete equally, however,

*Patriarchy, in this use, refers to rules (written and unwritten) of a social system which govern the power relationships between men and women. These rules expect particular behaviors of men and, consequently, require particular practices of women.

when they come from declining communities with low-paying jobs and disintegrating community institutions. Women cannot compete equally when they have inadequate support for their child-rearing responsibilities. Affirmative action, therefore, provides inadequate advocacy for people who live with the two conditions which are most responsible for the poverty of female-headed households: declining neighborhoods and child-rearing.

According to William Julius Wilson, the decline of black inner-city neighborhoods was set in motion by historic racial discrimination, or discrimination which occurred prior to the era of civil rights.[15] Racial discrimination created a division of labor in which blacks occupied the lowest of agricultural and manufacturing jobs. This division of labor was intensified due to macroeconomic processes since World War II. Many blacks had left low-paying agricultural jobs in search of better-paying manufacturing jobs. As the number of agricultural jobs reduced, blacks migrated within the United States and became concentrated in inner-city areas. When blacks migrated, their easily identifiable race made it possible for employers to hire them in the lowest levels of the economic structure.

After World War II, blacks largely stopped migrating to the inner city. As migration slowed, the black neighborhoods became younger as new births populated the community. As frequently happens when the age of a population declines, the structures which held in place the values, traditions, and institutions of older, more stable generations began to change. In addition, manufacturing declined. Jobs in manufacturing were replaced by very low-paying jobs in the service sector or by management and professional jobs. Middle-class blacks left the inner city in search of management and professional jobs in the suburbs. In the inner city, the presence of a high percentage of youth, the absence of the most qualified and stable workers, and changing institutional structures allowed room for higher rates of crime, more out-of-wedlock births, and fewer skilled workers and professionals.

One of the most significant losses in a declining community is the loss of support by the community and business sector for the public school system. A public school system without adequate community resources leaves young people without training for higher-paying jobs and without the kind of hope for the future which motivates them to invest in long-term goals. Communities also lose interpersonal networks through which young people learn to find job.

Communities which are plagued with these conditions become "socially isolated" and "socially dislocated," two conditions which severely curtail the ability of individuals to compete equally for jobs. The inner city is socially, economically and interpersonally *isolated* from the outside world. Cut off from jobs and stabilizing institutions, the inner city creates its *social dislocation*, a "civility" of violence, drug trade, and teenage pregnancy, short (late teen age) life expectancies, and no future. Wilson occasionally calls these dislocations "social pathologies." Women who have worked and lived with inner-city black women respond to Wilson that teenage, out-of-wedlock pregnancy is "normal" in these situations. In fact, a body of literature has developed which celebrates teenage pregnancy as an exercise of a poor adolescent woman's right to choose. Such "choices," which may be normal and understandable for young people who are trying to survive in desperate situation, are unlikely to lead to positive, stable futures for communities and individual lives, especially if U.S. domestic policy maintains its present direction.

Wilson's analysis demonstrates why few men or women in declining communities are helped by the philosophy and legislation of equal rights, access, treatment, and opportunities. He seeks to reverse this decline through macroeconomic policies which would produce jobs. He does explicitly support some prongs of a family policy. His framework for analysis, however, considers race and class but ignores gender. His policies do not extend far enough to insure that our poorest female-headed households would benefit equally from this economic development.

Ignoring the factor of gender, Wilson *assumes* that middle-class female-headed households can usually escape poverty.[16] This assumption, however, is contradicted by other data. According to Mary Jo Bane and David Ellwood, half of all new spells of poverty* in female-headed households begin with a change in family structure, and the majority of households on welfare are not part of the black underclass but are white.[17] To escape poverty, single, middle-class mothers, regardless of color, must either have adequate independent resources to maintain their lifestyle or they must be able to compete equally in the job market. Most mothers must struggle to achieve either. Many female-headed households are created from families who are barely middle-class with two full-time workers; other female-headed households arise from middle- and upper middle-class families whose resources are inadequately distributed between the new households. In these cases, the poverty of the female-headed household is related more to gender than to race or class. Community disintegration, therefore, cannot explain the high rate of poverty among female-headed families in general, most of whom are white and do not live in the inner city.

All mothers have difficulty competing well in the job market because of the historic sexual division of labor. The private division of labor holds women primarily responsible for care of the household and for the emotional and economic responsibilities of raising children. The public division of labor assigns a lesser value to "women's work," so that, *as a group* women have consistently earned about 60% of what men earn. Gender expectations in marriage, divorce, separation, and out-of-wedlock pregnancy magnify the impact of both the public and private inequities.

Gender, by definition, is not primarily a matter of biology; gender refers to the socially-defined expectations, patterns, duties and obligations which are attributed to a person because of his or her biology. Middle-class women in the United States traditionally have been expected to marry, to bear children, to remove themselves from the workforce in order to become the primary parents to children, to keep house, to

*"Spells of poverty" refers to the periods of time for which a person is poor. Persons may be "relatively" poor (less than ten years) or "absolutely" poor (more than ten years).

be volunteers, to get "jobs" rather than to have "careers," to care for the extended family and the community and give priority to the husband's career. Men are expected to be self-sufficient, to care for a family economically, and to win prestige and status. In marriage, women generally receive economic assets and men gain relational supports. Most couples, even dual-career couples, invest most heavily in the husband's career. These norms may be even more stringent among lower middle- and working-class couples. These couples have traditionally needed two workers, but the woman's job is frequently part-time and does not carry the benefits (pensions, insurance, health care plans, etc.) of the man's job. Therefore, most husbands accumulate economic earning power which a wife can never reach if she drops out of the work force to devote her time to pregnancy and child-rearing.

The economy of marriage anticipates a "private transfer" of material and relational benefits between men and women. "Private transfer" means that money earned by one spouse is used to benefit both. Private transfers occur daily when, for example, one spouse buys groceries for both. Assets which benefit both spouses, such as equity in a house, furniture, and investments, are now usually considered the property of both. The most valuable forms of marital property, according to Lenore Weitzman, are not daily expenses or the assets accumulated during a marriage but those assets which contribute to future earning power: education and training, seniority which brings an increased base for salary and benefits, the goodwill value of a business or profession, the entitlements to company goods and services.

Divorce destroys this private transfer system. Divorced men and women rarely volunteer to support one another after divorce; instead, the state intervenes to recommend a child support and/or maintenance system. Furthermore, women have the primary emotional and economic responsibility for children after divorce, even when men pay child support. Women generally retain custody of children, and child support awards rarely cover half the support of a child. When single women are employed full-time, they must either pay the high cost of child care or depend on friends or relatives to provide primary care. Women who are awarded child support are also primarily responsible for collecting it. Many women have felt emotionally and financially defeated when faced with a court battle which could only result in minimal support. The problems with private transfers are even more complicated in the case of out-of-wedlock pregnancy. After a divorce, men are far more likely to remarry than women, allowing men to regain the caring of marriage but further weakening their financial resources.[18]

Women's secondary place in the socioeconomic structure, the problems of private economic transfers, and the difficulties of being fully available for full-time employment make all but a few mothers vulnerable to poverty after divorce. These structural inequities, rather than divorce itself, explain why middle-class women are vulnerable to poverty. In addition, these factors were solidly in place at the time of a rise in the divorce rate and divorce law reform. Therefore, the situation was ripe for an increase in the poverty of women and their dependents.

I am not saying that men do not suffer emotionally and financially after divorce. Men may, in fact, take a longer time to recover emotionally from a divorce since they tend to become more relationally isolated; they also experience immediate economic consequences. Individual men, especially in those situations where the couple needed two incomes to make ends meet prior to a divorce, may discover that divorce is extremely difficult financially if they maintain their responsibilities toward their children. As a group, however, middle- and upper-class men have a running start in the "equal" competition in the job market because of the frequently intangible economic privileges they are able to accumulate.

Affirmative action has not failed, but its benefits most easily help those persons who are most readily able to compete in the economic market. For the increasing numbers of persons who do not compete easily, either because their community resources have not prepared them adequately for the demands of the workplace, or because the requirements of work conflict with responsibilities for dependents, affirmative action is not enough.

The Rhetoric of Self-Sufficiency as Public Policy Response

The 1960s rhetoric of equality, which developed during the rise of individualism, convinced the nation that all individuals had the right to compete equally for jobs. A derivative of this rhetoric, the belief that all adults should be economically self-sufficient, has pushed 1960s individualism to its extreme form. "Self-sufficiency" gained prominence as a norm for public policy during the reform of divorce law; it has also become a norm for welfare reform. As such, the societal expectation of individual, economic self-sufficiency now structures the lives of poor women and children. It requires that unmarried women, whether or not they are mothers, be fully self-supporting; regardless of any other responsibilities, economic independence must now be a mother's first goal. It ignores the fundamental interdependencies which allow children, women, and men to survive and thrive.

In divorce reform law, self-sufficiency for both spouses serves as the basis upon which either spouse would be rewarded support or maintenance. In middle-class situations in which men are economically self-sufficient and women are not, the requirement creates a new norm for women and replaces the traditional legal expectation that men will support their wives throughout life; the opposite norm, that men and women will share in the emotional and practical responsibilities of caring for children, is more difficult to enforce. The new law recognized that three groups of women would need help toward the goal of economic self-sufficiency: those with full-time responsibility for young children, those who required transitional support to become self-supporting, and those who are incapable of becoming, or are too old to become, self-supporting.[19] Unfortunately, in contradiction to its intention, some studies report that the actual financial awards to mothers of young children declined both in value and in number.

In welfare reform, the goal of making women "self-sufficient" is clear in the renewed push to "get women off the rolls and back to work." "Work," however, is defined as employment; private domestic labor, or child care at home, is not considered work. Under terms of the new 1988 law, as summarized by Andrew Hacker, mothers who depend on welfare must take any "bona fide" job or get job training once their children reach the age of three.[20] These norms of immediate self-sufficiency do not help a woman plan for her long-term economic security, nor do they provide for adequate child care. The welfare reform bill allocates about $6 per day for a mother's child care needs and has not created the 1.5 million new child care placements which are needed in order to enforce the new law. I find it ironic that a poor woman who is able to find a position caring for children in a child care institution is considered "self-sufficient," but a poor woman who cares for her own children in her own home is considered lazy and in need of being "disciplined" into self-sufficiency by public policy. Hacker finds it disconcerting that most of the policy makers are white, but many of the welfare recipients are black; is it not equally disconcerting that most of the welfare legislators are male, but most welfare recipients are female?

Self-sufficiency has gained widespread political support because in one word it expresses the ethical motives and goals of both contemporary political conservatives and liberals. Ironically, these motives are diametrically opposed. Liberals still seem to think that self-sufficiency is a route to liberation and equality, while conservatives hope that self-sufficiency is a road to entitlement cuts.

The proponents of self-sufficiency in divorce reform were middle- and upper middle-class liberals who failed to distinguish between civil and economic equality. They reasoned that women had a right to compete equally for jobs and seemed to be exercising that right by entering the workforce in great numbers. Women *wanted* to be employed, so women *should be able* to support themselves. On the basis of this conclusion, they intentionally changed the fundamental moral basis of the law from retributive justice to distributive justice.

According to Weitzman, the old divorce law was founded on a religious moral principle which supported marriage by punishing guilty spouses and rewarding innocent ones.[21] This principle, formally called "retributive justice," means that the harm done to individuals and society is reconciled or justified when the guilty pay. Retribution, as a genuinely *religious* ethical principle, has been under suspicion at least since Jesus challenged the law of "an eye for an eye." Jesus never demanded retribution but said, "go and sin no more." Jesus was more concerned that the vulnerable be cared for than that the guilty pay. By eliminating retribution in favor of distribution, therefore, the framers of divorce law potentially advanced the theological ethical basis of the law. "Distributive justice" is concerned with the sharing and dividing of human goods for human welfare.[22] Not recognizing the difference between civil and economic justice, the reformers implicitly defined distributive justice as "equal competition for jobs" rather than "care for the vulnerable." In this way, economic self-sufficiency fulfilled the liberal agenda and left the door open for conservatives to withdraw social supports from women and children.

Self-sufficiency appeals to political conservatives because the individual, not society, is held squarely responsible for life's problem. Warren Copeland, in *Economic Justice: The Social Ethics of U.S. Public Policy*, points out that the value conservatives uphold above all others is liberty.[23] The conservative economic agenda supports the liberty of free markets which supposedly provides a healthy economy in which all should thrive. A woman's poverty, one must conclude from conservative principles, results from her poor exercise of her freedom. Therefore, the poor are not deserving of entitlement programs, and such programs are not economically healthy. The self-sufficiency reasoning of liberals in divorce law reform is easily converted into a kind of self-sufficiency in welfare reform which supports the conservative agenda. The rhetoric of self-sufficiency also blurs the distinction between psychological self-esteem and sociological realities. A sense of personal competence and self-reliance *is* necessary for people to change their living situation. The Divorce Law Research Project asked judges whether they expected "mothers of preschool children to stay home with the children, or to go back to work to earn money," and the judges echoed what many divorced mothers have themselves said: the judges thought that it was "good" for a divorced woman to be economically self-reliant rather than dependent on her husband and that it was "healthy," a form of rehabilitation which would help her build a new life. Psychologically, a woman going through a divorce may gain a strengthened sense of self through economic independence and a widened circle of colleagueship and contribution outside the home. She will also discover the social realities of mothering and competing for a job in a market economy. Individuals need to try various combinations of socially important work; they also need the opportunity to readjust their vision of their personal quest in relation to their experience of social limits. Even though the need for self-reliance is psychologically valid, this psychological reality does not create socioeconomic equality.

Social opportunities are different from social requirements. Self-sufficiency as a norm *requires* that a single mother be employed outside the home full-time and mother full-time. An opportunity allows a single mother to coordinate her responsibilities for family and employment. The requirement ignores the family in favor of employment. Poor women get requirements without opportunities. The judges held that the yoking together of employment and motherhood was normal and reasonable, a value judgment which is consistent with historical expectations of poor women but contradicts the structure of gender in the United States for middle-class women, especially those women who married and raised children in the ultraconservative fifties. The judges also expected that former husbands could not fully support their ex-wives, a situation which is often the case but which depends upon the income of the husband. Oppression for either gender occurs when social limits are set so low that individuals' potential far outweighs their social possibilities; it also develops when social expectations are set so high that individuals' personal effort cannot possibility attain what society considers normative.

The rhetoric of self-sufficiency confuses civil and economic equality, liberal and conservative political agendas, psychological needs and sociological realities, opportunities and requirements. Although poor female-headed households differ in their problems and need various kinds of help, self-sufficiency does not give them a language with which to appeal for that help. "Natural rights" and "equal opportunity" were forms of rhetoric which gave the oppressed a voice; they represented principles to which socially vulnerable people could appeal in order to transform the society in which they lived. In contrast, "self-sufficiency" is a principle which denies poor women and children a voice; it represents a rhetoric which socially powerful people use to create unrealistic expectations of poor women. Like the rhetoric of equality, the rhetoric of self-sufficiency is brilliant, necessary and tragic. It is brilliant because it creates an unlikely political alliance; it is necessary because it appeals to the sense of hope which is often lacking in the poor; it is tragic because it ignores the social realm which family and employment must share.

If Not Economic Self-Sufficiency, Then What?

The policymakers who reformed divorce and welfare legislation have written into law the expectation that mothers will be employed and raise families. This lifestyle as normative is one for which many feminists have hoped. How are we to interpret this change as it becomes a central norm for policy and law? Some policymakers might suggest that policy is responsive to the desires of women; others, more cynically, might grumble, "they asked for it; now they'll see how much they like it." Women should not be fooled, however, by the belief that this new norm heralds progressive change. The norms of work and family differ radically for poor and middle-class women. Traditionally, policy has been structured to reinforce the norm that middle-class women will have economic support if they remain at home with their families and do not pursue employment; similarly, policy has required poor women, particularly single-parent mothers, to maintain families while engaging in low-wage work. Social security attempts to provide some poor mothers, notably widows, with middle-class options. One must question whether the norms which have traditionally governed the poorest women are now being pushed upward into a middle-class female population. The norm that mothers will be employed and raise families can be considered progressive only when mothers' domestic labor is recognized as work which contributes to society, and when family policy provides the support base for single mothers' employment.

In addition to the changes in family law which restructure middle-class gender in public policy, gender is being restructured in the social imagination of young women in the United States. The greatest obstacle Sidel's self-sufficient adolescents will face is not the animosity of individual men or women but the rules of the workplace which create conditions which require that mothers without household support will be employed under the same standards as men who have traditionally had the services of women as their household supports.

Are the rules of the workplace changing? Some industries that are dependent on female labor are instituting policies which support women's employment, but these efforts presently reflect the efforts of individual industries rather than widespread change. Furthermore, sociologists are beginning to report that male "innovators" who modify these rules experience workplace discrimination similar to that of women.

If the norm which expects a woman to be employed and raise a family is to lead to progressive rather than punitive legislation, the rhetoric of equality must catch up with women's practices. Women, I contend, will continue to challenge one another with practices in the family and the workplace which carry different expectations of what women's equality means. The practice of such diverse commitments to women's equality has helped to create a situation in which gender may be restructured in the United States. "Competitors" will continue to help women gain cultural and political power. "Innovators" will help women and men gain the kind of workplace flexibility which allows fathers and mothers to care and to work. "Heroines" will challenge the belief that women should choose between family and employment, or that men should neglect their families to give "110%" in the marketplace. "Survivors," who have increased so substantially in number, challenge more privileged women to realize that civil equality alone will never insure mothers' flourishing; rather, measures which provide basic economic equity must remain a part of women's policy agenda. The care of single mothers and their children, and therefore, the possibilities of their equality and their flourishing, can only be insured through the interdependencies of the government, the local community, the family and the individual. The language of self-sufficiency is inadequate to this task as an analysis of its logic will make clear.

CHAPTER 3

The Logic of Self-Sufficiency

All families must fulfill two roles: a nurturing/child-rearing role and a provider role. . . . Husbands usually work [*sic*] fully if they are not disabled. . . . Wives sometimes work [*sic*] fully but, more commonly, they work part time or not at all. They usually cite family responsibilities as the reason they do not work. The provocative question is, Do we want single mothers to behave like husbands or like wives?

David T. Ellwood[1]

Traditionally, women have lived with two alternatives for organizing their lives. Most women have lived privately, within the household, and have devoted themselves to domesticity. Some women have become public leaders. These women have frequently forsaken the family, have received support from domestic servants, or have combined work and family with great interpersonal and social tension. Occasionally, groups of women have tried to develop a third alternative which mediates the extreme split of the public and private life, but after a period of experimentation women have been pulled back into the two original alternatives.

These two alternatives, the private life or the public life, are rooted deep in western consciousness. Many feminists argue that the division of private and public life developed under modern capitalism. While modern capitalism reenforced these two alternatives, it did not create them. These models have a hold on women of at least two and a half millennia, rather than two and a half centuries. If we unearth these models and reflect upon them critically, we will be less entangled in their stranglehold.

For these reasons I will now draw into these reflections two figures who may at first seem to be unlikely conversation partners in a dialogue about the role of women's self-sufficiency in U.S. domestic policy: Plato and Aristotle. Plato and Aristotle described two alternatives for organizing women's relationship to public and private life which remain the primary options for women's lives even today. Less than coincidentally, Plato and Aristotle were great proponents of self-sufficiency. Furthermore, Plato and Aristotle influenced Christian theology and religious practice, so that these two alternatives have dominated women's way of being religious. If the norms for mothering are to include *both* family *and* employment, a third alternative must be found—one which enables women and men to have a full range of choices for integrating their private and public lives.

Individual Self-Sufficiency and Personal Responsibility

Self-sufficiency encourages personal responsibility. This assumption undergirds much of the reasoning of people who want poor women to pull themselves up by their bootstraps and of people whose only model of women's equality suggests that women must compete in a male world for male power without relying at all on men. A model which promotes the idea of the political equality of women and men of aristocratic classes was outlined by Plato in *The Republic*. In this book Plato developed a conversation between his teacher, Socrates, and a number of Socrates' companions, about the way a just city should be organized. In a just city, women and men of the aristocratic classes could be equal if they were self-sufficient. People could be self-sufficient if they were educated to understand the responsibilities of freedom, if they renounced their domestic attachments, if they took full responsibility for the conditions of their own lives, and if they allowed compassion to enhance the wisdom of their own judgment. Self-sufficiency allowed women and men to search for and achieve the "life of contemplation," a life which released them from menial tasks. The conditions of self-sufficiency in Plato's just city suggest a normative way of thinking about human potential, desires, and responsibilities which holds dire consequences for the poor and for all parents and children. The first condition of self-sufficiency is that equal people must be free. Plato did not believe that a free person had the right to do as he or she wishes, as many contemporary Americans do; rather, a free person was one who has mastery over his or her emotions and was governed by reason. A person could only be reasonable, however, if he or she had been educated. Once educated, Plato argued, women would be free and self-mastered. Educated women ought to be able to govern just as educated men did.[2]

Plato seemed to advance the cause of women when he advocated women's education. In fact, history has proven Plato's point: all movements for the advancement of women have included large programs of education. But what was the content of this education? When Socrates asked his companions "Can women be equal to men?," Plato assumed that women's equality would be achieved when women could be educated to play the game (governing, making war, and philosophizing) on men's turf (the battlefield and the Senate) under men's rules. Using this definition of equality, Plato actually denied the possibility of equality for several groups of people. First, those people who were not educated for freedom could not, by definition, be equal. Applying Plato's reasoning to contemporary times, many poor people with scattered educational histories, including some of America's most famous female activists, such as Sojourner Truth, are by definition not equal. Second, Socrates' conversation partners raised the question, "if women can do what men do, can men do what women do?" Should men take on the domestic tasks of the household? Socrates, however, was unwilling to talk about that question, claiming that it makes the story too long.[3]

Plato did not value the tasks of the household enough that men should also consider participating in them. He was unwilling to acknowledge that the life of contemplation and public action was not self-sufficient but has depended upon the labor of women and slaves who were necessarily unequal. Plato ignored the problem of the just distribution of domestic and public tasks between men and women and among classes for a particular reason. He recognized, however, that even free and equal men and women could not survive if they did not have food, shelter, children, and economic relationships. He also knew that ownership—close ties to particular property or people—created inordinate self-interest which often destroyed equality. He proposed a second condition of self-sufficiency: the renunciation of all attachments among aristocrats. Parents would not know who their children are; children would be raised in common; property would be held in common. Under the first condition, domestic tasks were devalued by Plato; now, all family life was eradicated.

Plato required, in Jean Bethke Elshtain's words, "the high price" of women's equality: the sacrifice of personal attachments, particularly the mother/child relationship.[4] Elshtain fails to note, however, that men must pay a price by sacrificing their property. Furthermore, Plato's plan would also require that men forego fathering and that women never become property owners. The possibility of men's intimate parenting and women's economic independence were not issues for Plato as they are for us. Plato's observation, however, is just as true today as it was 2500 years ago: attachments to children and property give rise to relational power for women and economic power for men. He was skeptical that free and equal persons would ultimately use this power fairly. Since people abuse their relational and economic power, Plato believed that the only way to guarantee justice among women and men was to eliminate all personal relational and material attachment. In other words, in order to maintain the possibility of freedom and equality, he eliminated the family.

Plato proposed communal childrearing among aristocrats, but he also devalued children because they were not full moral beings. The devaluation of children was necessary in order for Plato to maintain his third condition for self-sufficiency: the self-sufficient person must realize that he or she is totally responsible for his or her own life. Plato, however, was quite aware that people's choices are limited by their environments. Unlike present-day proponents of self-sufficiency, Plato squarely faced the contradiction between a person's total responsibility and the limits of choice within his or her social environment. In order to hold people totally responsible for their choices while recognizing the limits of their environments, Plato executed some fancy mythological and theological gymnastics.

In the Myth of Er, which concludes *The Republic*, Plato allowed Er to observe life after death in order to satisfy mortals' curiosity about the afterlife.[5] Er discovered that after death, the soul would face its most important choice: the choice of the next environment in which it would live. This literary device allowed Plato to admit that a person's environment makes a huge difference in the kind of life that person will lead. A person's environment molds his or her character in ways which shape a person's capacity for wise or unwise choices, and every environment makes some opportunities available while eliminating others. For that reason, the between-life choice of an environment is the most important choice an individual can make. Throughout, Plato recounted various examples of souls which had chosen wisely or unwisely and the consequences they faced.

As people who do not usually believe in between-life choices of a next life, contemporary Americans are likely to protest that we are born into a set of circumstances of life which are beyond our control, even though as adults we may transcend those circumstances. This problem is an obstacle over which Socrates would have stumbled, had he been willing to engage its most obvious contradiction: that newborns, who are without reason and choice, cannot be considered responsible for their life's circumstances. The story of newborns, Socrates claimed, "is not worth repeating."[6] Plato considered the plight of the newborn unimportant, just as he thought domestic work insignificant. Plato's trivializing of women and children is significant in light of the three points he wanted to drive home. First, the person is responsible for the pursuit of justice and the moral choices he or she makes. Second, one of the moral choices a person makes is the choice of an environment in which he or she lives. Third, the person alone is responsible for this choice; the gods cannot be blamed. In other words, Plato could only maintain his emphasis on personal responsibility by ignoring the fact that a child at birth does not have control of the circumstances of life which will shape her formative years.

So far we have discovered that Plato was a great advocate of personal responsibility, pushing the possibilities for responsibility to the extreme: the human being is not only responsible for the choices she makes but is responsible for the environment in which she finds herself. In order to maintain his belief in personal responsibility, Plato created a purgatory in which that choice is made. Furthermore, he could only maintain this ideology of total personal responsibility by creating an image of God which has had a profound and enduring influence in Christian theology: the self-sufficient and just God. Plato emphasized personal responsibility for theological reasons. The actions of the Greek gods, he believed, were immoral, yet humans justified their own immoral behavior by claiming they were imitating the gods. Only a just God, according to Plato, deserves to be imitated. The only God who can be just at all is transcendent, omnipotent, unchangeable, invulnerable, and unswayed by the vicissitudes of human desire or necessity. This God is self-contained, a God of divine self-mastery. This just God deserves to be imitated.

Plato's ideology of self-sufficiency offered his readers an ideal toward which to live. Plato, however, was also deeply aware of the suffering in which some people live. For example, should society have any compassion for Theresa and Hillary? What are the implications of compassion in a just world in which all people and God are responsible for themselves? Plato was quite aware that if we are compassionate, we open ourselves to experiencing the suffering of others. He raised many concerns about how experiencing the suffering of others can distract one from the pursuit of justice. A good man who witnesses the grief of another person may feel his own grief more acutely. When he takes pity on another, he is more likely to take pity on himself. Some people even get vicarious pleasure from witnessing the suffering of others. These reactions may cause a person to lose control of himself, to lose his reason. When we suffer, Plato suggested,

> we need to think about what has happened to us. One must accept the way the dice fall and then order one's life according to the dictates of reason. One ought not behave like children who have stumbled, wasting time wailing and pressing one's hand to the injured part. Instead, the soul should learn to remedy the hurt forthwith, to restore what has fallen, and to remedy the complaint with the appropriate medicine.[7]

Ultimately, Plato was not suggesting that we simply ignore or deny our own suffering, but that we recover from our anguish privately by thinking it through. In fact, in the Myth of Er, Plato seems to have had a positive attitude toward experiencing the suffering of others. Some souls who choose unwisely have not experienced enough suffering to understand the consequences of their choices. Compassion, however, was only secondarily for the sake of the sufferer. As his fourth condition of self-sufficiency, Plato maintained that one's compassion primarily provides knowledge with which one may make wise decisions about one's own life.

In our society today, as in Plato's ideal republic, well-educated women, who can compete like men, are declared free and equal. Plato's woman of the aristocratic class has several contemporary versions. She is able to compete in the traditional male world because she has been relieved of some of her traditional responsibilities. Unlike Plato's women and men, however, she does not earn public help by virtue of her social contribution but she employs domestic help at great cost to herself. Like Plato, she may decide that her responsibilities for her work and for family represent an irreconcilable conflict of interests which requires her to sacrifice one or the other. Either way, when we promote this vision as the primary route to women's equality, we, like Plato, promote equality for some women while ignoring equality for those women with less education, status, prestige, or money.[8] We, like Plato, ignore the fact that women's domestic labor supports public life; even worse, we devalue the efforts of women who attempt to support families with meager resources.

Plato, however, was more astute than we are; he imagined, as our policy makers have not, that the full equality of women and men in even one sphere requires a radical change in social structure. He abolished family life, not so much to free women from domestic labor for service in the public sphere, but because men and women abuse the power which comes with material and personal attachments. Modern society has offered dramatic proof that Plato was right about human nature. Men and women abuse the power they have with one another and with people who are socially and economically less powerful. In divorce litigation, society grants to men the greatest portion of economic power and to women the greatest portion of relational power. At their worst, fathers abuse this power by not supporting their children financially, and mothers abuse this power by denying their children a direct relationship with their father. Across class lines, those with social, economic, and relational power refuse to share this power with poorer families, demanding instead that poor families not be "dependent." People whose mothers and fathers were nearly poor and who are newly-monied, including generations who have emerged from the U.S. working classes into the managerial classes, are often the least compassionate toward the sufferings of others.

In our obsession with self-sufficiency, we may be well on our way to enacting a portion of Plato's structural change, the abolition of the family and the destruction of attachment, without any of the benefits to the common good which Plato hoped to achieve in his just city.

Communal Self-Sufficiency and Economic Necessity

Plato was considered the friend of women because he argued that aristocratic women could be equal to men under some conditions; in contrast, Aristotle has been seen as a enemy of women because he argued that, by nature, women and slaves were inferior to men and, therefore, were unsuited for public life. Aristotle's particular views on the nature of women and slaves were adopted into Christianity through the writings of Thomas Aquinas in the Middle Ages and have had a profound influence on patriarchal arguments which claim that "woman's place is in the home." Aristotle is important to this study because he described the dominant alternative to Plato's conclusions: the belief that women are inferior to men, not only due to their biology, but also due to economic necessity. Aristotle connected women to domesticity, not by valuing its reciprocity with the public realm, but by normalizing the economic constraints which limit women's activities.[9]

Aristotle's idea of women's subordination to men due to economic necessity provides a sobering backdrop against which to read his comments on friendship—some of the finest in western literature—in the *Nichomachean Ethics.* Philosopher Martha Nussbaum calls Aristotle's idea of friendship "communal self-sufficiency."[10] Unlike Plato, whose idea of self-sufficiency allowed for little vulnerability, Aristotle opened up the possibility of being ourselves while being present for others—what Nussbaum calls "appropriate vulnerability." Such vulnerability allows a friend to be a person whom we enjoy, who is helpful in times of need, and who holds us accountable for our actions. Many people today long for such a friendship and count themselves blessed if they have one. Aristotle observed, however, that friendship can only occur between people who are free and equal. When people are bound by economic necessity, as are husbands and wives and slaves and masters, they can no longer be equal friends; one must be superior to the other.

Plato recognized the mutual stake that equal men and

women have in relational and economic power and advocated that both be sacrificed, but Aristotle dissolved this intricate power balance. Instead, he suggested that women are bound to men by *economic necessity* because they are inferior, and men, as superiors, are obligated to women by *moral duty*.[11] Neither philosopher entertained a third alternative: that women and men might share freedom, equality, and economic means if they share relational and economic power.

In a relationship between unequals, Aristotle argued, justice is created by the reciprocal obligations of the parties. The superior individual, the husband or the master, who has more status, privilege, and power, is obliged to use these benefits to care for the inferior individual, the wife or slave. The inferior individual, in return, is obliged to accord to the superior friend the honor which is his due. This understanding of reciprocity between unequals, husbands and wives, undergirds the traditional idea that husbands are morally obligated to provide economic support for their wives, and wives are required in turn to provide household labor, including sex, for their husbands. This understanding of the relationships between economic and moral obligation provided a foundation for family law which dominated family obligations from Aristotle until the 1970s, when divorce reform legislation helped to eliminate Aristotle's assumptions from family law.

Many people seek a relationship like Aristotle's friendship in marriage and family life. As contemporary Americans' desire for intimacy in marriage has increased, our emphasis on marriage as an economic relationship has decreased. Some definitions of marriage and family, which are used in policy discussions, have affirmed the affective qualities of marriage while ignoring the economics of marriage. Aristotle helps us see how our desires for the equality of men and women in marriage—and for "communal self-sufficiency"—fall apart without an understanding that marriage and family life is both relational and economic. The tragic flaw in Aristotle's ethic lies in the assumption which is its cornerstone. Even though the bonds of moral obligation on the part of the "superior," economically-privileged party loosen, the economic necessity of the "inferior" party remains intact. This theoretical problem in Aristotle's ethic corresponds exactly with the practical problem that impoverished mothers are facing today, on both societal and personal levels. When society no longer considers itself responsible for poor families, and when privileged men are not obligated to support their children, the raw vulnerability of poor children and their mothers is exposed.

In an ironic turn of thought, however, feminist philosophers have begun to retrieve Aristotle on behalf of women, not because of his statements about women's nature, but because of his philosophical method. Nussbaum suggests that Aristotle's method of observation leads him into a "conflict of appearances" which causes him to change his mind.[12] For example, if we followed Aristotle's methods in thinking about U.S. welfare policy, we would "go to the source": talk to welfare mothers, observe their households and communities, record the contradictions of their lives, and discover the ways in which our policies are or are not suited to their situation. Nussbaum quips that if Aristotle had observed women as closely as he observed shellfish, he would have come to a different conclusion about the equality of women!

Self-Sufficiency and Early Christian Theology

The ideal of self-sufficiency as the goal of good Christian living entered Christian theology through the synthesis of Hebrew faith and Platonic thought which is called Neoplatonism. The Hebrew God is characterized by deep, passionate love and sorrow over humankind's waywardness. God's mercy is revealed when God is tempted to destroy people who are unfaithful but is moved by the pleas of Moses. God is just when God tenderly cares for the widow, orphan and other poor, and when God expects God's people to do the same. This God is very different from the platonic God who is "transcendent, omnipotent, unchangeable, invulnerable, and unswayed by human vicissitudes of desire or necessity." Jesus had affirmed the Hebrew law, "You shall love the Lord your God with all your heart, soul, and mind, and you shall love your neighbor as yourself."

Early theologians, under the influence of Plato's thought, were gripped by the idea that one might love God and find justice through the contemplative life. Their life of worship and prayer led them to search for a "beatific vision" or mystical union with God. Even so, they deviated from the Greek ideal in some important ways. The Greeks sought "the good life," or a life which conformed to justice, but the Christians sought "perfect love," the life which expressed the love of God and neighbor. The Greeks assumed that social inequality reflected a natural difference in the worth of persons, but Christians believed that a spiritual equality—"neither male nor female, slave nor free, Jew nor Greek, but all one in Christ Jesus"— transcended social inequalities which would be erased in the future life with God. The Greeks had debated whether the good life was found in the life of action or the life of contemplation, but never considered whether a life of justice could be found in the life of menial duties. Christians affirmed that the life of perfection could be found in all three walks of life—the walk of contemplation, of action, or of necessity— even though they suggested that life of perfect love could be found more easily in some walks of life than in others. Christians, unlike the Greeks, raised the question of whether a life of perfect love could be found equally in the life of necessity.

Early Christians struggled to interpret the meaning of neighbor love in relation to the practice of the contemplative life. Some believed that the love of God could be expressed primarily through works of piety: prayer, worship, and the practice of contemplation. Others believed that the love of God was expressed through works of mercy: almsgiving, caring for the sick, or caring for the poor. Some thought that one could express the love of God in the family as well as in acts of care for the neighbor. Christians who differed with one another sought one another's counsel, wrote treatises in favor of particular positions, and created a variety of practices which reflected their religious commitment. Their debate became intense, at times even vociferous, for much was at stake: they believed that the correct practice of the commandment was of utmost importance for their ultimate salvation. As Christianity developed an orthodox position, Christians were increasingly taught that life in the family was a distraction from the Christian's ability to practice perfect love.[13]

Social and political events of the 4th century helped to determine the orthodox Christian position. Prior to the 4th century, Christians had been persecuted. A Christian's ability to maintain her fidelity to her faith, despite deprivation or even torture, was evidence of her salvation. After Constantine converted to Christianity and persecution of Christians ceased, Christians sought a new way of proving the strength of their faith. Christian orthodoxy affirmed that faith and salvation were more secure in a life of sexual and economic renunciation. Theologians such as Jerome and Chrysostom exalted the life of virginity. Although Christians practiced virginity in a variety of lifestyles, the monastery or the convent became the primary institution which made the life of virginity possible.

According to historian Elizabeth Clark, Jerome and Chrysostom considered celibacy not only a *politeia*, a distinctive walk of life, but also a *philosophia*, an embodiment of philosophy.[14] Chrysostom considered monastic life to be a realization of just social organization, a modification of Plato's *Republic*. Although Chrysostom rejected Plato's specific proposals for the equality of women and men, he incorporated the conditions of self-sufficiency into the monastic lifestyle.

Chrysostom and Plato agreed that women and men could lead a superior life if they renounced personal family ties, including sexual relations as a spouse, affectional relations as a parent, and property or wealth which allowed family life to sustain itself materially. The theologians published the disadvantages of marriage, taken from Greco-Roman literature, which included, for a woman, "pregnancy, a crying baby, the tortures of jealousy, the cares of household management, and the cutting short by death of all its fancied blessings," and for a man, "anxieties over a wife, children, slaves, problems with money and in-laws, the sickness and death of loved ones."[15] The ideal of renouncing family ties, even when it meant the abandonment of children, was based on the belief that family responsibilities created a conflict between loyalty to God and loyalty to the family. "Too great affection (for one's children) is a lack of affection for God," wrote Jerome. He commended a mother who was grieving the death of her children because she "thanked the Lord for freeing her from a great burden."[16] Affectional and economic renunciation was the primary criterion of freedom: freedom from the bondage of marriage and the economic and affectional responsibilities of family life. Just as women and men became equal in Plato's *Republic*, equality between women and men in the monastery, Clark argues, depended upon squelching not only sexual desire but also gender identity.

Just as Plato's aristocratic women could achieve the greatest possibility of equality through sexual and economic renunciation, monastic women fared well as women outside the family. Monastic life provided opportunities for education and some degree of self-governance. Women could enter monasteries and avoid being forced into unwanted marriages, and sexual renunciation allowed women to avoid life-threatening pregnancies in a time when birth control was unpredictable and women often died in childbirth. While this renunciation allowed women to have a greater degree of self-sufficiency than married women, monastic women often had men as spiritual and moral guides and mentors.

Just as Plato imagined that people could choose their lives and their environments and, therefore, be totally responsible for the harm that befell them, Jerome urged the individual to withdraw from earthly contingencies by choosing the holy, ascetic environment instead of marriage. Environment was as important as sexual renunciation, for Jerome objected to the lifestyles of Christians who combined elements of the environments of monasticism and marriage, such as the *subintroductae* who cohabited with the opposite sex without sexual relations. For Jerome, no human needs or environmental hardships would warrant male-female cohabitation because "it seems to me that living with a woman entails a certain pleasure."[17] Jerome and Chrysostom urged individuals to enter the monastic environment regardless of any environmental contingency.

Plato's self-sufficient individual could improve his or her choices through experiencing compassion with those who suffered, but he or she ultimately gained union with the eternal through detaching himself or herself from human contingency. Even though Jerome's ideal monastic life incorporated the pietistic love of God with the compassionate love of the neighbor, this early Christian neighbor love distinguished its interpretation of the Great Commandment from later Christian thought in two ways. First, the practice of perfect love was usually guided by a hierarchy of love which could not be reversed. The ultimate union with or contemplation of God was the goal of works of mercy or neighbor-love. As Augustine would later say, "the active life is the stirrup of contemplation."[18] Love of the non-personal, non-familial neighbor was valued more than love of family; in fact, what might be called domestic "works of mercy" were not only expendable but a distraction from the love of God.

Second, a Christian's works of mercy for the neighbor served the Christian's own salvation and eternal reward, rather than serving the neighbor in need for the neighbor's sake. For example, the narrative of the *Life of Olympias* is filled with the tales of Olympias' almsgiving and charitable deeds. These tales are sandwiched between the narrative of her ability to escape a second marriage and the narrator's conclusion that her life of charity has served the primary goal, the attainment of such purity as unites her with God. The narrator closes with the writer's underlying motive: the hope that the writing of Olympias' biography might serve to benefit the writer's eternal reward.[19]

Although Jerome's version of Christian asceticism offered a striking comparison to Plato's self-sufficiency, the story of the early church's position on virginity usually concludes not with Jerome, but with Augustine, the African bishop of Hippo. Augustine is commonly blamed for the church's disdain of sexuality, but his position is much more subtle than that of Jerome. Augustine became celibate in his mid-thirties and a spokesperson for the church's position on marriage and sexuality in his mid-forties. Augustine had spent his early adulthood under a mix of contradictory influences. Living in a culture which idealized male friendships and having lost his father, Patricius, in his late adolescence, Augustine sought the intellectual and spiritual companionship of like-minded men. In this search he became an *auditor*, or pupil, among the Manicheans, a dualistic sect who disdained the body, sexuality, and procreation. He also lived in a monogamous relationship with a nameless concubine, with whom he fathered a child about whom he later writes tenderly and sensuously. Significantly, he chose to live in a celibate religious community after he renounced his concubine in order to marry prominently, a marriage which never took place as a result of his religious conversion. Later he wrote that fidelity, rather than legality, makes a marriage:

> This problem often arises: If a man and a woman live together without being legitimately joined, not to have children, but because they could not observe continence; and if they have agreed between themselves to have relations with no one else, can this be called a marriage? Perhaps: but only if they had resolved to maintain until death the good faith which they had promised themselves. . . . But if a man takes a woman only for a time, until he has found another who better suits his rank and fortune: and if he marries this woman as being of the same class, this man would commit adultery in his heart, not towards the woman he wished to marry, but towards the woman with whom he had once lived.[20]

Augustine's loving relationship with his concubine may be as significant for medieval forms of marriage as Luther's marriage to Katherine von Bora is for modern marriage. When Augustine looked back on his early adolescence and his forsaken relationship from the vantage point his later celibacy, he "was inclined to judge them gently," according to Peter Brown.[21] This gentleness pervaded Augustine's later attitude toward marriage, virginity, and other relationships which bear resemblances to later forms of marriage which I will call "medieval compromises." In his middle years, death and social disorder, rather than sexuality, became for him the primary problems against which humans must struggle. Sexuality became problematic not in and of itself, but as it created divisiveness within self and society. Augustine remained convinced that celibacy led to a more harmonious life, but he defended marriage, rightly ordered, as a reflection of a harmonious, godly society. Augustine's gentler attitude toward marriage, however, contained a caveat: a rightly ordered marriage, like Roman society, was strictly patriarchal. Unlike Jerome and others with more strictly ascetic views, Augustine no longer promoted the ideal of spiritual, although hierarchical, friendship with women. The possibility of life in sexual relationship, as a defensible although secondary Christian lifestyle, was bought with a price: the submission of women to men in the "harmonious" social order.[22]

Medieval Practices: Compromises Between Family and Virginity

Christian ambivalence about family life was reflected in both theology and practices which flourished in the Middle Ages. Although some early and medieval theologians disdained marriage and the life of necessity, a minority of theologians found equal value in marriage and celibacy. In the highly romantic 12th century, for example, monks wrote that Christians could increase their love for God in marriage and the family as well as in the monastery.[23] Some influential theologians, such as the 13th-century theologian Thomas Aquinas, accorded a positive but secondary value to marriage.[24] Christian orthodoxy, however, never considered marriage and the family equal to or preferred to virginity as a Christian lifestyle. This Christian ambivalence manifested itself in at least three medieval practices.

Child oblation was the practice of donating a child to a monastery to be raised. Child oblation served both religious and socioeconomic purposes. As a religious offering, a child who was donated to celibate life gained a spiritual and ecclesiastical reward on behalf of a parent who might not want to seek celibacy for himself or herself. Parents might contribute both the child and a financial donation. Generally, children did not leave the monastery once they were oblated. This restriction benefitted both parents and the monasteries: parents were not held responsible for the support of an adult oblate who chose to forsake religious vows, and monasteries could depend upon the economic resources and adult services of the child oblates they had raised. When oblates had a difficult time living within this agreement, they were occasionally released to secular life, but frequently they had to remain in monastic life against their will. As a socioeconomic practice, child oblation helped families regulate family size, consolidate inheritances, and thereby provided for the security of the family household. Oblation provided economic security, status, and education for poor children. Oblation represents a compromise between marriage and celibacy because, as a form of adoption, it suggests one of the ways that monasticism incorporated the tasks of family life into the life of celibacy.[25]

Celibate marriage was the opposite compromise: it brought the ideals of sexual renunciation into marriage and the family. Celibate marriage was practiced by both clergy and laity from the fourth to the 12th centuries. Marriage partners who desired to pursue a celibate ideal either vowed to abstain from sexual relations while continuing within the economic relations of the family or remained married but sought the opportunities to enter separate monasteries toward the ends of their lives. Religiously, married celibates gained some of the status and merit which were associated with vows of monastic celibacy. Celibate marriage, however, also served many practical functions. Women sometimes initiated celibate marriage when they had been forced by their fathers to marry against their will or when their health could not sustain pregnancy and childbirth. The church benefitted economically when clergy who were celibate and married bore no children who could claim property, dowry, office or support from the church. For both spiritual and practical reasons, the church made several attempts create a celibate clergy, even to the point of attempting to separate married clergy from their wives. Some persons who recognized this threat to marriage invoked Jesus' prohibition against divorce so that clergy and their family were not separated by force. When clerical celibacy was imposed in the 12th century, the practice of celibate marriage among laity fell into disfavor.[26]

Concubinage was a compromise between marriage and celibacy which allowed for sexual and affectional relations within one partner's primary covenantal fidelity to God and the church. In ancient Roman practice concubinage, or nonmarital cohabitation, had two forms. Occasionally, partners temporarily cohabited, but primarily, concubinage was practiced by those men and women who wished to live in a permanent, affectionate relation as husband and wife but were of different social classes and, therefore, were unable to marry. One situation in which partners were considered socially unequal existed when one partner was consecrated to God. The Christian Roman emperors limited the rights of concubines and their children, making concubinage an inferior form of marriage. Christian theologians added their own religious ambivalence about sexual relations to the debate about the status of concubines. As an array of legal problems developed regarding the needs of concubines and their children for economic support, medieval canonists gave concubines and their children a variety of economic rights and legal statuses, depending upon whether the children were born of a legitimate marriage, born of a concubine and a layman, or born of a concubine and a priest.[27]

Plato and Aristotle had presented contrasting possibilities for women's place in the social order. The ideals and practices of Platonic self-sufficiency, which became institutionalized as monasticism, dominated the church for almost 1500 years. The complexities of life, including people's spiritual, economic, sexual, and affectional needs, invariably modified the ideal and practice of self-sufficiency. The sexual and economic renunciation which made the practice of self-sufficient ideals somewhat possible "cohabited" with families' inevitable connection with one another and with the social order. Through oblation the church provided support for unwanted children; through celibate marriage partners cared for spiritual, emotional, and health needs; through church law which responded to concubinage, children and their mothers without full legal and social status were cared for. Self-sufficient ideals were ultimately set aside by Martin Luther, who anticipated that a Christian vocation of marriage would increase the possibility of care for poor women and children.

CHAPTER 4

Luther's Alternative to Self-Sufficiency

I stared in bewilderment. Yes, it was true that my father had
not come home to sleep for many days now and I could
make as much noise as I wanted. Though I had not known
why he was absent, I had been glad that he was not there
to shout his restrictions at me. But it had never occurred to
me that his absence would mean that there would be no
food.

Richard Wright[1]

Women—or mothers? When women are primarily seen as
mothers, some women contend, their social contributions go
unrecognized. When mothering is ignored, others argue,
many of women's significant contributions and challenges
remain unaddressed. Mothering is too frequently romanticized or neglected, both by women of various ideologies and
by general culture. When we value women's vocations in their
fullness, we can illumine the struggles of mothers within
various situations of oppression without assuming that
women who mother are somehow better or worse than
women who do not mother. For many women whose broader
social opportunities are limited, including poor women of
many times, places, and geographical locations, the opportunity to choose mothering represents a line of demarcation
between hope and despair.

Tucked innocuously between parts of the story of Joseph
in the Book of Genesis is a tale of mothering that most of our

Sunday School classes probably skipped. The tale goes like this: Tamar was a young women whose husband, Er, the son of Judah, the brother of Joseph, died early, leaving no children. According to the Hebrew custom of Levirate marriage, she was then given in marriage to Er's brother, Onan, that she might become a mother. Onan, aware that her children would be considered the children of Er rather than his own, refused to inseminate her. When he died, Tamar had no children, so she should have been given in marriage to the next brother, Shelah. But Shelah was not yet of age, so Judah suggested that Tamar be cared for in his house for the time being. Eventually, Tamar realized that Judah was procrastinating. Thinking she was barren, Judah did not intend to give Shelah in marriage to her.

Tamar dressed as a temple prostitute, with a veil over her head, and attracted Judah's attention at the city gate. He wanted to sleep with her, and she asked in return that he pay her with a goat and leave his seal and his staff as collateral. After they had intercourse, she donned her widow's dress and returned to Judah's house.

When Judah sent the goat, he asked for the prostitute at the gate but he could not find her. He inquired among the neighbors, fearing that his honor would be impugned if he did not pay, but the neighbors maintained that there was no such prostitute. About three months later the neighbors told Judah that Tamar had behaved as a prostitute and was pregnant. Judah called for her to be burned for fornication, as was the custom; but when she appeared, she handed Judah his seal and his staff and said that the father of the child was the owner of these items. "She is more in the right than I am, because I did not give her my son Shelah," Judah repented.

Tamar bore twins. During the birth, the hand of one twin emerged, and the midwife marked it with a thread; then the hand was withdrawn and the second twin was born and named Perez. Then the first twin was born and named Zerah.

In the popular lore of Christendom, this story is about Onan, who "spilled his seed upon the ground." For Martin Luther, who expounds on it at length in his *Lectures on*

Genesis, the story is about the exploitation of Tamar, a poor woman.[2] Judah, according to Luther, denied Tamar her rights. Although Judah took Tamar into his household and gave her basic sustenance, he deprived her, against her own wishes, of the honor of motherhood, the right to preside over a household, and firm economic security.

Tamar, for Luther, is not a victim, but a moral agent. The neighbors have been outraged by Judah's actions, but he is a man of such power that no one can try to reason with him. So they plot with this powerless woman to claim what is rightfully hers, even when it means that she must sin boldly. She has the support, protection, and even the advice of the community; in collaboration with them, she chooses to engage in the seduction and incest. In the human world, her actions cannot be excused. Technically, she has sinned twice: deceiving Judah and engaging in incest; but Judah has sinned once: denying her right to motherhood. But in God's world, in which grace upsets the relationships of the powerful and the powerless, she is more righteous than Judah.

Then, in a moving passage of interpretation, Luther describes the agonies of the breach birth of twins. Tamar's pain and exhaustion, Judah's tearful prayers, and the near death of mother and twins, are the prolegomena to the miracle of the shifting of the fetuses and the healthy childbirth. In Luther's interpretation, there is no hint of the easy explanation: Tamar's travail as punishment for her sin. Instead, Luther's admiration and empathy for Tamar pervade the passage. This story, Luther concludes, is given to us for our consolation. It contains no moralism, no record of sins for which God expects payment. Rather, this story of Judah's abuse of his power, of the community's action to right the wrong, of the brave choice of a poor woman, and of the near-death of mother and children in a long-awaited birth, is nestled in the crucible of God's grace. Luther's recovery of motherhood as a radically graceful life changed the social landscape, and the theological presuppositions, of the 16th century.

Luther: Agent of Change

In the early 16th century, women's lives were in flux. The medieval compromises, which had provided some measure of equity for women, were disintegrating. Since the 12th century, married couples had been discouraged from practicing celibacy, reducing women's options for regulating their reproductive lives. Concubinage, with its legal and economic benefits, was growing into disfavor among the church hierarchy. The oblation of boys had ceased, but girls were still placed in monasteries with little opportunity to return to secular life if they wished. Although these and other medieval practices declined, the Renaissance brought new interests in the human person and his or her expressions in art, in sexuality, in science, and in trade. Into this late medieval world came a variety of religious reformers who prepared the soil of culture for the growth of the modern age. The pivotal reformer was Martin Luther.

Martin Luther bridged the old and the new worlds. As a medieval thinker, he deplored social chaos and believed that disease, death, and violence signified the presence of sin and evil in the world. True to the curiosities of emerging German humanism, however, Luther took great interest in the forces which motivate the human person. The person was more than his or her psychology, however; the person was embedded in reciprocal relationships in the family, the local community, and the church.

As a practical theologian, Luther sensed the intimate relationship between the church's economic practices, its spirituality, and its theology. Luther believed that the prevailing theology of the church, a theology of merit which rewarded people according to their good works, encouraged pietistic practices which impoverished women and children. In the give and take between his observation of the practices around him and his growing understanding of the divine-human relationship, he developed a new theology of grace and the common life which challenged the exploitation he witnessed around him. This challenge led to a shocking reversal of women's way of living a religious life.

Luther did not set out on a campaign to change women's lives. As Luther attempted to harmonize his beliefs about Christian lifestyle and his understanding of God's grace, however, he so aptly verbalized the concerns of the people that his writings became a lightning rod for action. In this way Luther's faith lived beyond him, creating his rhetorical boldness and his fear of social chaos, extremes which are evident in his behavior and thought. First in his monastic life, then as a reformer, and finally as a husband, father, and pastor, he passionately embraced God's cleansing grace; with equal fervor he doubted his experience of God. Expressing the grace he found, he befriended the poor and abandoned, denounced Papal power, exploitation and greed, and openly and outrageously reported on men's and women's bodily desires. He developed new norms for Christian living: he pronounced God's blessing on sexuality, parenting, domesticity, and labor; he reinterpreted the meaning of spiritual poverty; he did not hold individuals solely responsible for their environment but advocated a life of compassion toward the neighbor for the neighbor's sake. His new theology reversed the tenets of self-sufficiency in favor of mutuality. When he doubted God's grace, however, he underestimated and feared the power of the movement for which he had been a catalyst.

Luther: The Aristotelian Option?

Luther is known as a patriarch. In his classic work *The Family, Sex, and Marriage in England, 1500–1800*, the historian Lawrence Stone charged that "the triumphant emphasis on patriarchy as one of the benefits of the Lutheran Reformation is here unmistakable."[3] Stone argued that Luther's position on women reversed the educational gains women had been making during the advent of humanism. Some feminists have pointed out that Luther's efforts to empty the convents diminished women's options for a life which was freer from male domination than marriage, a life under women's control and in relationship with other women.

Furthermore, Luther taught that sex was a "conjugal duty," robbing married women of a significant tradition through which women could regulate reproduction. Formerly, if women wanted to abstain from sex in order to diminish childbearing, they could call on church tradition which held that "too great a love of one's spouse" was sinful. Finally, Luther hung these beliefs around a hierarchical framework, what I have called the "Aristotelian alternative" of women's natural and necessary subordination to men.[4]

Luther, however, was hardly a disciple of Aristotle. Luther's argument for "justification by grace through faith alone" reviled the Greek philosophers, whose influence on medieval theology Luther held responsible for the theology of works which he found so destructive. Luther claimed, in fact, that "virtually the entire *Ethics* of Aristotle," which include Aristotle's chapters on friendship, was "the worst enemy of grace."[5] Even so, Luther's hierarchical understanding of gender relations was startlingly like that of Aristotle. Luther claimed that in a well-ordered world, husbands have authority over wives, parents over children, and masters over servants. For Luther, like Aristotle, these were not strictly oppressive power relationships but a reciprocal whole. Superior parties have moral obligations toward inferior ones: superior parties must treat inferior parties well, sharing wealth, wisdom, and disciplining fairly; inferior parties respond by honoring those who have provided for them. The moral obligation which holds the reciprocal relations of superior and inferior together reflect Paul's body metaphor: the power given to the superior part is balanced by the honor given to the inferior parts.

Luther did not share Aristotle's uncritical acceptance of this hierarchy, however, because he also observed that exploitation occurs when the moral obligations of the hierarchy break down. Without moral reciprocity, the authority of the superior party disintegrates. In place of wise authority, the raw power of the superior party exploits the inferior for its own selfish gain. Luther's early works form a commentary on this exploitation. He noticed those who are most vulnerable in the breakdown of hierarchical relations: women and children. Without this vision into the exploitation which occurs due to the breakdown in hierarchical relationships, Luther's theology would never have become significant. Martin the monk would never have become Luther, the theologian of radical grace and the historically significant reformer of culture the world knows him to be.

Economy, Spirituality, and the Criticism of Exploitation

Luther's experience of God's radical, unearned grace conflicted with his experience of exploitive practices of religious life in the monastery and on his pilgrimage to Rome. Claiming that the greed of the church was destroying its spirituality, Luther sought to expose the economic corruption of the medieval church. Rome had devised many ways of collecting revenues in return for reassuring people that their salvation was secure. The most famous of these methods was trade in indulgences and relics which produced a thriving business in the dispensing of eternal merit by Rome. As a result of the Pope's promise that eternal reward could be purchased, many fathers embarked on pilgrimages which took them away from their responsibilities in the home and community; pilgrimages took large portions of family provisions as well. Luther himself had made such a pilgrimage and had attempted to buy eternal reassurance; he decided that the idea that the Pope could grant eternal reward for such "pieties," at the expense of the children, wives, and local communities at home, was a sham. Early in his writings, in 1520, Luther wrote "To the Christian Nobility" about the poverty of families and communities which resulted from the Pope's deceit:

> Such people think that going on a pilgrimage is a precious work. . . . God has not commanded it. But God has commanded that a man should care for his wife and children, perform the duties of a husband, and serve and help his neighbor. Today a man makes a pilgrimage to Rome and spends fifty, maybe a hundred, gulden, something nobody commanded him to do. He permits his wife and child, or his neighbor at any rate, to suffer want back home. And yet the

silly fellow thinks he can gloss over such disobedience and contempt of divine commandment with his self-assigned pilgrimage. . . .

If a man . . . vow to make a pilgrimage . . . for the sake of a good work . . . [let] priest and master show him how to use the money . . . for God's commandments and for works a thousand times better by spending it on his own family or on his poor neighbors.[6]

Luther charged fathers with abandoning their families and their communities as they sought religious merit. He held the Pope and his priests responsible for the theological teachings which promoted these practices, claiming that the Pope ignored the poverty of families by encouraging the laity in false and expensive practices of piety which satisfied the Pope's own greed.

Luther also charged that the Papacy had manipulated theological teaching in order to absolve the Pope of his responsibility for the support of the dependents of clergy. The clergy took vows of celibacy, poverty, and obedience which gave the church the first claim on their time, effort, and money, but the practice of these vows did not keep clergy from having families. Many pious priests, Luther claimed, had only one "shame," the genuine love of a woman: "From the bottom of their hearts both are of a mind to live together in lawful wedded love. . . ." Priests lived in intimate relationships which were increasingly considered illegal by canon law but, because of the faithfulness of the love, were marriages in God's sight.[7] The celibate priest with wife and child, however, was not helped to provide for them.

Furthermore, the vow of poverty led many clergy to mendicancy, or begging, and left many poor clergy families. Luther protested that poverty in and of itself was not a spiritually superior state and was not an exercise of the Great Commandment; it simply served the Pope's power.[8] Calling upon the teachings of scripture and the practices of the early church, Luther urged the Pope to legalize the families of priests and to make provisions for poor clergy and their dependents so that begging could cease. The Pope would not agree to this more equitable lifestyle, Luther concluded, because "greed is the cause of this wretched, unchaste celibacy."[9]

Having exposed the tentacles of the Pope's greed, Luther then developed a defense of priests' relationships with women:

> Not every priest can do without a woman, not only on account of human frailty, but much more on account of keeping house. But if he keep a woman, and the pope allows that, and yet may not have her in marriage, what is that but leaving a man and a woman alone together and yet forbidding them to fall? . . . The pope has as little power to command this as he has to forbid eating, drinking, the natural movement of the bowels or growing fat. . . .
> . . . when the estate of matrimony has been entered against the pope's law, then his law is already at an end and is no longer valid. . . . [10]

While it is tempting to decry Luther's acceptance of priests' needs for women as domestic servants, it would be misleading to do so. Luther described a widespread practice of the time which, he claimed, was exploited by the church. Human beings, Luther wanted to argue, do not simply need domestic service and employment; rather, they have fundamental needs for sex, affection, companionship, as well as physical care. Relationships between priests and their servants frequently developed toward fuller relationships. When church law denied the full reciprocity of physical, moral, economic and sexual commitment in these relationships, exploitation was inevitable.[11]

Full caring relationships were also inhibited by compulsory vows of poverty, Luther argued. In "The Judgment of Martin Luther on Monastic Vows," Luther claimed that true obedience and poverty are found in faith and service of the neighbor, rather than in vows which, in the name of being a good work attributed to one's salvation, separate one from the neighbor.[12] True spiritual poverty, he claimed, does not seek one's own poverty but employs one's provisions for the welfare of one's neighbor. When people take vows of chastity and poverty in order to pursue the spiritual life, these vows conflict with faith. Theologically, these vows violate the principles of Christian freedom and perpetuate works-righteous-ness, causing people to deny service to Christ their neighbor. Practically, vows impede family members from taking on economic responsibilities for other family members, such as a son caring for aging parents, a parent providing a dowry for a daughter, or a priest caring for his children. Compulsory vows are also contrary to common sense and reason about the natural sexual and relational inclinations of the human.

This criticism of exploitation and Christian practice led Luther to formulate his doctrine of Christian freedom. Luther has been accused of preaching Christian freedom, but know-ing nothing of liberty. Luther is often judged by enlightenment or marxist notions of freedom though he, of course, had the benefit of neither discourse. Under the conditions of his time and using the cultural ideas available to him, Luther developed a new idea of Christian freedom which represents one of the great ethical turning points in western civilization.

In 1520 Luther argued for "The Freedom of the Christian": "The Christian is perfectly free Lord of all, subject to none; the Christian is perfectly dutiful servant of all, subject to all."[13] Christian freedom or liberty means that "faith alone justifies, frees and saves." Christian freedom is a necessity because all are helpless to live up to the commandments. None are self-sufficient. Since Christians are free from works for the sake of salvation, they are free to offer works of mercy to the neighbor *for the neighbor's sake*. Christian freedom has a purpose: a saving faith produces works which enhance, rather than detract from, human relationships.[14] Practically speak-ing, Luther declared Christian freedom from the institutions which embodied economic and relational renunciation. The-oretically, Christian freedom replaced self-sufficiency with a primary concern for human relationality.

Luther's observations, then, caused him to break with the dominant modes of ecclesial thought and practice of the time. If God's freely-given grace was the gospel's fundamental mes-sage, then caring for the poor families and communities, rather than empowering the rich church at the expense of women, children, families, and communities, had to be theology's practical norm. Against the Aristotelian tradition which disdained domesticity as inferior, and often subhuman, work, and against the Platonic tradition which understood sexuality as sinful rather than God-given, Luther granted a status to domesticity and sexuality as valuable, essential elements of human life. He wanted the church to recognize what he believed the God of scripture proclaimed: that economic equity, sexuality, partnership, and neighborly support further God's reign over God's good creation.[15] In doing so, he recalled theology to its Biblical heritage, and he created a new theological ethic of care.

Sexuality, Motherhood, and Children

In contrast to the Platonists and Christian Neoplatonists who implicitly degendered women in order to develop a semblance of equal, intimate, spiritual relationships with them, Luther proposed a vision of male-female intimacy based on gender difference as a "divine ordinance." Gender difference has proven to be an ambiguous norm for women. The idea of gender difference has been used to promote dividing the world into two spheres, the male and the female, the public and the private, and relegating women to the private realm. For Luther, domesticity was not privacy; rather domesticity involved the total, indivisible world of love and work.[16] Unfortunately, the idea of divinely ordained gender difference, taken from Luther and joined with later socioeconomic forces which moved livelihood outside the household, did help to relegate women to the privacy of the home. Luther's idea of gender difference, however, was more complex than the simple equation of public and private with male and female spheres; in fact, it created a new theological anthropology, or understanding of the human in the divine-human relationship.

In Luther's view, gender difference was divinely ordained because gender was an expression of God's creation, the human body.[17] Challenging the dualistic anthropology of the Greeks, he argued that the body and soul could not be split between reason and desire; rather, reason and desire constituted an organic unity in Christ. This contention allowed him to value sexuality, domesticity, and childbearing in a new way, even though the body, disease, death, sin and evil were deeply connected in his culture. He was able to value women in their reproductive world, rather than only valuing women when they escaped that world. Sexual urges and desires were no longer to be denied but were a God-given part of the realm of creation. The here-to-fore invisible realm in which women and children often lived could not be taken for granted and was not expendable.[18] No longer "not worth mentioning," children and childbearing represented the good fruit of sexuality, intrinsically of worth in and of themselves. As delightful members of the family rather than economic assets at best and encumbrances at worst, children were not to be ignored or disdained by theology. In his willingness to value children in this way, Luther became a prophet of the modern age. The idea of childhood, not as miniature adulthood but as a time of life in which immature individuals have distinctive needs, grew in favor in the centuries after Luther.[19]

Luther believed that God-given sexuality was an essential part of theological anthropology. Sexuality served relational, as well as procreative, purposes. He defended women as sexual beings and linked their sexuality with women's natural right to mother. Marriage, he thought, was the institution within which sexuality and parenthood could be best facilitated; therefore, he thought that almost all people should marry. On the basis of these reflections Luther linked the church's economic exploitation and a reformulated anthropology which understood sexual desire to be a natural component of the human. So, when a young nun appealed to Luther to end her involuntary confinement to a convent, Luther demanded that convents release those women who were held against their wishes and took on the responsibility of helping the women find husbands.[20] The few people who were called to voluntary celibacy, Luther taught, did not gain merit for their piety but acted out of grace.

Although Luther advocated the relational purposes of sex

within marriage, he also defended men's and women's equal right to sexual relationships outside marriage for procreative and sexual purposes if the spouse were sterile or unable to engage in sexual activity. In response to women who were unable to conceive within marriage or whose husbands were unwilling to bear children, Luther approved of Levirate marriage.[21] When his opponents claimed that he was giving women too much sexual license, he reaffirmed his position, suggesting that now that he was "less timid" he could affirm Levirate marriage under some circumstances for both sexes.[22] The position often attributed to Luther, that of a moralist who believed that sexual relations could only occur in marriage, clearly is called into question by this position. Although Luther did not advocate promiscuity, he argued (at least implicitly) for a 16th-century equivalent of artificial insemination and surrogate motherhood, without the benefit of modern technology and without disdaining human sexuality. His willingness to give this kind of pastoral guidance shows the extent to which sexuality and motherhood were controlling values in his theological anthropology. Most significantly, Luther believed that the human context in which sexual relations occur, rather than the legalities of marriage, must be of primary concern.

It is important to be clear that the pastoral problem Luther was trying to address was not a legal argument about rights, but a theological argument about the fundamental understanding of the human. Luther's problem was not the problem that contemporary women face: whether women should be able to *choose* to be or not to be mothers. This way of framing the women's problem depends upon the premises of enlightenment rationalism and modern individualism to which we, but not Luther, are heirs. Luther was fighting a battle which is a prerequisite for women's right to reproductive freedom, a battle over the theological understanding of the human: will sexuality and sexual expression be understood as a fundamental, God-given aspect of the whole human being? The nuns who appealed to Luther for help were oblated as young children as the result of a theological anthropology which understood that human urges for sexual expression were sinful and should be denied.[23] On the basis of his reformulated anthropology, Luther *assumed* that most women wanted to mother.[24] His complaint was against those church authorities who allowed a woman's destiny to be determined, not by her needs or desires to mother, but by the church's self-interested greed which distorted the image of the human in order to entice parents to place women in convents for the sake of the parents' eternal merit. Some commentators think that Luther urgently sought to find the nuns husbands because he feared their unbridled lust; but Luther assumed they wanted husbands, not only for sex and procreation, but also in order to become part of a household which could sustain their economic livelihood. Most of these women would not have the option of returning to their families!

Sexual Desire and Psychological Transformation

Theologians and ethicists have long since recognized the importance for ethics of Luther's radical dependence on God's grace, but they have failed to incorporate Luther's ethic of care into their interpretations of him. For example, moral philosopher Alasdair MacIntyre concludes dismally that for Luther "the events that matter all occur in the psychological transformation of the individual."[25] Theorists of the family have accused Luther of being responsible for creating a privatized, patriarchal family which separates itself from the public social order. Some forms of contemporary Lutheranism do emphasize individual conversion, social quietism, and the patriarchal nuclear family. Luther's passionate convictions about exploitation, however, indicate a far more complicated relationship between the individual, domesticity, and social and ecclesial change.

MacIntyre presents a terse summary of Luther's ethics in which he charges that Luther was only concerned about individual transformation, that Luther left no room for a positive understanding of human desire, and that, for Luther, our works were only the product of sinful desire.[26] From this summary we can extract three issues which challenge the argument I am making. First, if Luther truly abandoned reason in such a way that internal, psychological transformation is "all that matters," then his comments on economics and the family must be peripheral speculation and cannot have the priority I have attributed to them. Second, if human desire creates *only* a natural antagonism between God and humanity, then the human's sexual and material needs must exacerbate that antagonism and cannot possibly become part of God's good creation. Third, if works are only the product of sinful desire, then Luther's attempt to rectify economic corruption and relational injustice must be considered means to a theological end, rather than genuine attempts to challenge the corruption of the medieval church-state.

Brian Gerrish's explanation of Luther's use of reason provides a clue which resolves the second and third issues. Gerrish argues that Luther's reputation as an "irrationalist" is unjustified when one looks with precision at the ways Luther uses reason. Luther used the concept of reason in three ways. Luther disdained "arrogant reason," which he also called the "Devil's Whore,"[27] but advocated the use of "natural reason," which is an excellent gift of God, and "regenerate reason," a handmaiden of faith.[28] "Arrogant reason" believes that it can supersede the power of salvation by grace through faith by requiring works for salvation. Works, such as the vows of celibacy and poverty, become idolatrous in that they become more important than God's grace. Luther, however, seems to have been quite aware of the close interconnection between exploitive practice and a theology which justifies corrupt practice; one feeds the other, creating the idolatry of arrogant reason.

Luther based his argument for reform of the German nation not on arrogant reason, however, but on "natural reason." Luther affirmed the realm of the necessary. In Gerrish's interpretation, humans were created for domestic and civic (or political) occupations:

> What Luther terms the *communia*, the institutions of social life, were ordained of God. . . . With admirable common

sense Luther advises his flock to imitate the Biblical heroes
in their ordinary occupations, not in the special things they
did. . . .[29]

In these areas natural reason is "God's most precious gift" and
has a legitimate sphere of competence.

In his discussion of economic and relational corruption,
Luther used natural reason, as well as criticizing arrogant
reason, to make his point. He used natural reason when he
argued that the neglect of the family and the disdain of
sexuality were unacceptable results of the reigning theology
of works. As part of his argument, he pointed not only to the
source of the problem (arrogant reason), the Christian's attempt to purchase salvation, but to its consequence (natural
reason), the deprivation of the family economically and relationally. We can test this interpretation by asking whether it
would be acceptable to Luther if, as a work resulting from
grace, one neglected the family and disdained sexuality. Luther would have accepted the latter theoretically but with
skepticism as to its practicality. His theological anthropology,
guided by his natural reason, would tell him that God-given
celibacy rarely occurs. He would reject the former, arguing
that the actions of the grace-filled Christian are guided by the
sight of the neighbor and family in need: neglecting the family
or the neighbor is in contradiction to God's grace. He would
come to these conclusions by the use of "regenerate reason,"
which is natural reason illumined by the Spirit.[30]

This short examination of Luther's use of reason concerning economic and relational corruption suggests new responses to MacIntyre's charges. Natural reason has more
significance within Luther's thought than MacIntyre allows.
Natural reason is transformed into regenerate reason by the
reign of God in the realm of creation; together, they reveal
arrogant reason for the sham that it really is.

Luther would not agree that psychological, individual
transformation is "all that matters," regardless of corruption
in the world. Psychological transformation, when it is raised
to that kind of exclusive priority, becomes a new form of
arrogant reason. Luther would never agree that arrogant rea-

son ought to reign over natural reason, "God's greatest gift." Rather, economic and relational corruption initially motivates Luther's ecclesial criticism; therefore, theological interpretation, (regenerate reason) cannot take place without economic and relational reform (natural reason).

Furthermore, Luther would not agree that all desire is sinful; in fact, ascetic *denial* of desire antagonizes the relation between humanity and God. Natural reason led Luther to defend sexual desire and gender distinctions as an essential component of humanness. Luther would agree that *inordinate* human desire, which results in material greed or sexual licentiousness, creates antagonism between God and the human. He would also agree that material and relational *deprivation* results in a similar antagonism. Either extreme can distort God's good creation. Ultimately, the antagonism between God and humanity is created by the reciprocal relationship between inordinate desire, in the forms of avarice or licentiousness, and deprivation, in the forms of neglect of family or neighbor, or misdirected asceticism, secured by a theology of works.

Finally, Luther responded to the economic and relational corruption of his day by rethinking the theological justification of renunciatory practices, leading him to create a theological anthropology which incorporated desire. The new theology served an economically and relationally reformed society, one which ideally put the service of the family and neighbor at the center of its economic and relational practices.

The relational and economic context of Luther's theology prevents the interpretation that Luther was only concerned with individual transformation. Rather, his use of natural reason led him to incorporate relational and economic connectedness into the family and into society, not for the sake of family and society, but for the sake of God.

What Else Matters:
The Family as the Delight of God, or as Idol?

Luther's positive views on marriage and the family, which were dependent upon his valuation of sexuality and gender, are well-known as a predecessor to the modern "companionate marriage." In very general but stark terms, the difference between the modern companionate family and the medieval family line is a shift in cultural assumptions. In medieval culture people depended upon the family line to assure that the economic and other material needs of the family were met. Affection among members of the family line might occur but was not the primary force which bound them together. In contrast, in the companionate family the primary value and binding force is emotional bonding rather than economic survival.

While the shift to family intimacy describes an important shift toward modern living, the advocates of the intimate family have come under criticism from those persons, such as Richard Sennett, who attribute the erosion of public and social life to the emotional energy expended within the family. Sennett and others rightly criticize the family as idol: the kind of intimate family in which the family consumes all of its emotional and material resources without concern for larger social commitments.[31] His criticism of the intimate family, however, reads as if contemporary people must make a choice between commitments to larger society or commitments to the family. This way of construing the choices is misleading. It merely recapitulates the old choice between private and public commitments and leads us back into the same answer: men, and those women without children occupy the more privileged positions in society, and women with children are relegated to the realm of necessity.

Within the basic framework of Luther's thought the family is intimate but the family cannot be idolized. One cannot choose between family and society because through both, God is served. While Luther's willingness to understand sexuality and gender as good gifts of God led to his valuing of male-female intimacy, his new norms for familial intimacy were situated within his concerns for economic survival and for care of the neighbor in the community. His concerns also incorporated the education of the children and women as an important link between the family and the community. The family is a vocation, but the family has a vocation beyond itself.

What Else Matters:
Caring for Others and Resisting Exploitation

Luther's delight in the common life was rooted in his relationship with God. When one is freed by a saving faith, one does what is called for "in the normal course of events."[32] Faith is evident when "in the privacy of his own home a poor man, in whom nobody can see many great works, joyfully praises God when he fares well, or with entire confidence calls upon him when he is in adversity."[33] Out of this relationship with God the faithful are called to befriend the poor, regardless of what is to be gained from the alternative, cooperating with the rich and powerful.[34] The faithful are called to resist the abuse of spiritual power when it is used against the poor and powerless.[35] The faithful will not exploit the poor by exacting from them their already meager resources.

While Luther eloquently called for the resistance of the faithful when the church wielded its power against the poor, he troubles many interpreters because he does not seem to have applied the same ethic to secular governments. The poor, many have claimed, are left to suffer the abuses of secular governments gladly. Such a distinct separation between Luther's family ethic, church ethic, and secular ethic, however, does not do justice to Luther's thought. Luther's relational ethic guides the individual, family, the local community, the church, and the government.[36] When the care for the neighbor is shared reciprocally, the Great Commandment is most freely acted upon.

Inevitably, however, Luther also recognized what happens when this reciprocity breaks down. When people become too comfortable, for example, they tend to become lazy in their faithfulness. Then, the ruled suffer on earth and the wicked rulers suffer under God's righteousness. Out of suffering God recalls humanity to return to faithfulness. Although our human reactions of anger and hostility may provoke us to violence, our vengeance is to be tempered by a faithful and generous relationship with God and with one another.[37] Luther's character ethic also requires honesty and courage. One may incur suffering and persecution for the sake of God and neighbor. Faith in God may create a "bold, defiant, fearless heart that risks all and stands by the truth, no matter what the cost; he clings to the persecuted for the truth's sake."[38] When secular authorities intervene in matters of faith or act foolishly, this call to courage and honesty may require that Christians resist secular authorities.

Luther's willingness to care for the poor and to resist the exploitation of the church-state power calls into question his ambivalent response to the Peasants' Revolt. The reasons Luther gave for his response to the peasants are only somewhat consistent with his position on economic and relational corruption. The peasants, motivated by Luther's own courage against Rome, posted a series of charges against the exploitation of their own government.[39] In a rarely quoted section of his treatise, "Admonition to Peace," Luther agreed with the peasants' complaints; he also condemned the practices of the hierarchy, saying "we have no one to thank for this disastrous rebellion, except you princes and lords, and especially you blind bishops and mad priests and monks, whose hearts are hardened, even to the present day."[40] He warned, however, against the peasants' use of privately organized, physical violence.

His reasons for his position were eschatological: the vengeance of God is stronger than the vengeance of humanity.[41] Corrupt rulers ultimately would pay their debt to God. Luther suggested that, rather than resorting to physical violence, the peasants should suffer under the abuses of government while ignoring the laws which contradict the gospel—an assumption which leads Christians in the direction of what we would now call non-violent civil disobedience. As once he told monks and nuns that they could leave the convents and monasteries since they were held unjustly, now he suggested that in matters of the gospel, the peasants could simply "walk away from" the unjust laws of the corrupt rulers.[42] Consistent with his priority of helping the family or neighbor in need, he suggested that the peasants should better spend their time caring for one another than initiating violence. Like Augustine and Aquinas before him, he did not believe that the spiritual equality of the gospel indicated that all people should be social equals, and, consistent with his medieval assumptions, he also advocated that the peasants should pray about their own sins which cause their oppression.[43] He wanted to ease the plight of the peasants, but he was against violent means to reform. He did not agree with the peasants that "the end justifies the [violent] means." Later, however, he "accused himself of having the blood of these peasants on his head."[44]

Luther's reiteration that Christians should not kill and should love their enemies has tempted some Lutheran interpreters to emphasize "passive" suffering to the point that it gains such status that it takes on the quality of a meritorious "good work." For Luther, suffering was predominantly an active interim state which God rectifies in the eschaton, if not in historical social existence. One suffers under the abuse of others as an act of compassion; the side effect of this act is the creation of a stronger faith.[45] One suffers as a result of resistance in order to courageously defend God's rule. Luther's main concern in this situation was that a violent means is incompatible with a righteous end. Repeatedly in this treatise, he cited the suffering and abandonment of women and children during war as evidence of the truth of his concern.

Luther may have abandoned the peasants who looked to him as an ally; yet, adapted for our time, his thought is far more complex than the usual ethic of passive suffering. In our efforts to urge women to determine their own lives, those of us who have easier access to such self-determination should be reminded that passive suffering has been the only means of survival for many women. Walking away rather than fighting back may be some women's most advantageous response to the violence perpetrated against them. Even when they would be unable to do so for themselves, women may gather the strength to walk away because the treatment that their loved ones have received, personally and from governments, is ultimately contradictory to their understanding of the gospel. Luther's rather complex appeal to passive suffering is not without its psychological truth. Regardless of the ethical status we would want to attribute to passive suffering, we can join Luther in what I believe is a common goal: the restoration of the relationality expressed by the Great Commandment.

Replacing the Four Conditions of Self-Sufficiency with an Ethic of Care

When Luther recharted the theological map, he ultimately upset the conditions which support the ideal of individual self-sufficiency. First, Luther determined that the theology of economic renunciation served the Pope's avarice. In response to the Pope's theological and economic corruption, Luther no longer taught that sanctimonious poverty could produce meritorious works of mercy. Rather, since salvation was assured by faith through grace, a Christian's works of mercy were to be motivated not by concern for his or her own salvation but by love serving the neighbor for his or her own sake. Fundamentally, Christians should provide all people in need, including their enemies or the ungrateful, with economic support for their own sakes'. Christians were responsible for the care of the poor within their communities and for the education of children. Parents were to provide the economic support required by family life as part of a parent's vocation.

Second, Luther rejected the idea that relational renunciation, or celibacy as an act of piety, could gain merit toward salvation. He considered the involuntary oblation of children by parents unjust. After discrediting relational and economic renunciation, Luther taught that human sexual response and the affection and bonding which accompany it are a fundamental part of sexual relationships and of theological anthropology. He argued that almost all persons should marry, and he denounced those persons who disregarded women. Certainly, Luther assumed a domestic hierarchy which jars modern women. I am pointing, however, to the fundamental shifts in Luther's thought which created his ethic of care: first, Luther emphasized the value of sexuality and gender as a response to Rome's economic corruption; second, he not only denounced renunciation but gave the family a place of importance as a religious calling; third, he shifted the weight of religious opinion so that the Christian "minority" report, the idea that marriage was a lifestyle through which Christian vocation could be fulfilled, which had been part of the Christian tradition at least since Origen, became a majority report with its own possibilities and limitations.

Third, Luther's emphasis on salvation by grace through faith alone changed the terms of the debate over whether the individual is responsible for his or her environment in the search for salvation. On one hand, Luther no longer held that an individual's false choices were responsible for his or her walk of life; he fully recognized that exploitation by the powerful impinges on the individual and the family. On the other hand, the medieval Luther assumed that misfortune in some way reflected a person's sin. Under grace, however, an individual was free from undue concern about that sin to serve their neighbor. This shift called for certain affirmations and cautions. Luther's emphasis on working within one's situation in life could lead to a passive attitude toward transforming one's environment, as Plato feared. This passive attitude particularly developed when his admonition was combined with an eschatology which rewarded a person for coping with a bad environment without also supporting a person's attempts to transform it.

Luther, however, called for a more complex understanding of one's relationship to one's environment. First, a person may indeed find himself or herself to be living under unjust circumstances, not of his or her own individual making. Second, God and humanity cooperate in transforming those circumstances. God punishes the wicked with a punishment more stringent than human punishment. Because of God's justice, humans are freed for mercy. God calls forth strength of character as the exploited ignore unjust laws without harming others. Third, in transforming the environment, Christians renounce exploiting others or being exploited in order that the Christian may care for family and neighbor.

Finally, Luther denied that one should have compassion for others primarily for the sake of one's own salvation. In other words, he challenged the egotism of meritorious salvation. Instead, Christians are called to serve others because of the intrinsic worth of serving the neighbor in Christ. Service to others may result in the fulfillment of obligations towards one's family, in works of mercy towards one's neighbors, or in active suffering when one ignores unjust laws. When service to others results in active suffering, compassion is relational, for the sake of others. Strength of character enables compassion; compassion enables a stronger faith. Ultimately, one suffers compassion with family and neighbors for the sake of the rule of God.

In place of the ideal of self-sufficiency, Luther substituted an ethic of care. In response to the exploitation of women, children, and families, he developed a holistic anthropology which led to a fundamental web of interpersonal and institutional relationships. He valued domesticity, or the economic, sexual, procreative, and physical cares of the household, and he understood that care within the household is impeded or enabled by larger ecclesial and governmental practices. At the heart of his ethic of care was a renewed spirituality which was based on equity and generosity in all arenas of human relationships.

Luther's ethic of care, when joined with trajectories of the broader Reformation, had mixed results in developing practice. In place of the disintegrating hierarchy of church over the individual, Luther attempted to reestablish order around a domestic hierarchy guided by his ethic of care. This order, he hoped, would provide an environment for human flourishing. As the Reformation proceeded, Luther's domestic hierarchy evolved into an evangelicalism which lost Luther's generosity toward all people but retained Luther's hierarchy.[46]

Its hierarchy eventually divided domesticity into men's and women's spheres. This rigidly divided hierarchy has also proven unstable, once again exposing many women and children to poverty.

Luther developed a unique theology of domesticity out of the observation that church practice encouraged fathers to abandon their families. The poverty of men, women, and children, so important to Luther, exerted a very different influence in the theology of another primary Protestant reformer, John Wesley. Wesley provides a necessary corrective to Luther's ethic of care for the poor.

CHAPTER 5

Sexuality, Economics, and the Wesleyan Alternative

Luther's childhood illustrates the fact that adherence to an occupation, or rather an "estate," such as that of peasant, cannot remain a reliable factor in one's inner sense of continuity unless one is involved in the common hardships, hopes, and hates of that estate. These alone keep an ideology relevant.

Erik Erikson[1]

John Wesley shared Martin Luther's concern for the poor.* Although he lived two centuries after Luther, he also shared Luther's ecclesiastical struggle over the relative value of marriage, celibacy, and the family. As a practical theologian who endorsed "visiting the poor," Wesley frequently used the plight of poor women and children as a criterion for judging godly practice. Like Luther, Wesley was attracted in his early adulthood to the early church's emphasis on celibacy as a way of holy living; unlike Luther, Wesley incorporated the primacy

*I have chosen Luther and Wesley as representative theologians because the conflict between Christian vocation and domesticity figures intensely into their work. A more thorough and diverse conversation about the historical theology of poverty would necessarily include additional theologians who have yet to be read with close attention to their references to poverty, their observations of women and children, and ways in which these observations influence the theoretical framework of their thought.

of celibacy into his early theology. Only later in life did he admit that marriage and celibacy might be equally holy walks of life.

As a result, Wesley's early relational ethic was molded over an ideal of platonic self-sufficiency which he never totally abandoned. However, as a result of his concern for poor women, both among strangers and in his immediate family, Wesley's economic ethic moved beyond self-sufficiency toward an ethic of domestic economic interdependence. The empiricism of his theological method eventually led him into an Aristotelian "conflict of appearances" which caused him to modify his relational ethic and to develop an economic ethic which challenges contemporary models of economic self-sufficiency.

Wesley's Relational Ethic

Wesley's psychological ambivalence toward relationships of both sexual and emotional intimacy with women has been well documented.[2] Whatever the psychological reasons for his actions, Wesley was guided in his conduct of his relationships with women by the early church's neoplatonic lifestyle. The neoplatonic ideal of solitary self-sufficiency implied more philosophical and behavioral expectations than a simple aversion to sex; Wesley's neoplatonic streak required the same.[3]

The young Wesley found not only sex but all appetites to be an intrusion into his life with God. Wesley's asceticism, like Plato's, extended not only to sex but to eating, drinking and companionship. The nuances and limits of Wesley's asceticism, however, were hammered out in an intense correspondence with his father, Samuel, and his mother, Susanna.

The strict education and spiritual guidance given by Susanna and Samuel, to their ten surviving children is well known. Susanna had kept a strict educational schedule with each of her children, devoting regular and individual time to their literacy. The three boys and seven girls were educated equally at home, but the boys eventually completed formal schooling at Oxford. Even so, Susanna, Samuel and the siblings continued in prolific correspondence about many matters of importance.

The precipitating occasion for this round of intense family correspondence was probably John's suggestion to his parents that he would like to take Holy Orders. His parents suggested that he enter a time of self-examination. The overriding issue during the time prior to John's ordination in the correspondence between John and his parents was the extreme to which God requires asceticism in Christian service. The debate centered around the proper denial of one's bodily appetites: whether proper self-denial was represented by Thomas à Kempis' encouragement of more extreme forms of self-mortification or by Jeremy Taylor's more modified version of only thinking of oneself humbly. John rejected à Kempis' attempt to eliminate all joy from the Christian condition and wrote to Susanna that he respected à Kempis' piety but differed with him in some of his main points, particularly the idea that "God decreed that we should be perpetually miserable in the world . . . that the taking up of our cross implies our bidding adieu to all joy and satisfaction . . . that all mirth is vain and useless."[4]

Susanna agreed with John that perpetual misery and elimination of mirth is not the aim of the Christian. Susanna's reply, however, smacks of Platonism:

> As the happiness of man consists in a due subordination of the inferior to the superior powers, so the inversion of this order is the true source of human misery. . . . If the animal once get the ascendancy of our reason, it utterly deprives us of our moral liberty. . . . For any man to endeavor after happiness in gratifying all his bodily appetites in opposition to his reason is the greatest folly of all men. . . . Yet this is the case of most men. They live as mere animals, wholly given up to the interests and pleasures of the body. . . . He directs us where to place our joy, that it may be durable as our being; not in gratifying but retrenching our sensual appetites; not in obeying but correcting our irregular passions; bringing every appetite of the body and power of the soul, under subjection to his laws, if we would follow him to heaven.[5]

John seemed persuaded by his mother's moderation, and he attempted to find a more satisfying ethic in Jeremy Taylor's *Rules and Exercises of Holy Living*. Again, however, he found no room for the fruits of Christian assurance and wrote to his mother for comfort:

> But if we can never have any certainty of our being in a state of salvation, good reason it is that every moment should be spent, not in joy, but in fear and trembling, and then undoubtedly in this life *we are* of all men most miserable. God deliver us from such a fearful expectation as this![6]

Rather than the comfort of assurance from his mother, John received direction back to à Kempis' self-mortification from Samuel. Although Susanna has the reputation as the stern Wesley parent, Samuel seemed motivated to write by the possibility that John could be persuaded by the more modified nuances of his mother. After admitting that he was several letters in debt to his son because he did not know how to respond in a satisfying way to his son's concerns, Samuel defended à Kempis. Yes, Samuel said, men tend to extremes, à Kempis and contemplative men on one side and "the bulk of the world" on the other, but "For all that, mortification is still an indispensable Christian duty."[7]

In her next letter, Susanna responded to John's concerns about Taylor. She wrote that humility is

> the mean between pride, or an overvaluing of ourselves, and a base, abject temper on the other. . . . In proportion to the sense we have of God's infinite majesty and glory, and our own vileness and weakness. . . .[8]

John, however, rejected such Calvinist assumptions and wrote back to his mother, seeming to have resolved the issue for himself. He wrote that he agreed with Taylor concerning the knowledge of God and its relation to absolute humility but had reservations concerning the knowledge of the neighbor:

> But to judge ourselves the worst of all men implies a want of knowledge [of the neighbor]. . . . This kind of humility can never be well-pleasing to God, since it does not flow from faith. . . .[9]

The result of this correspondence with his parents was that John incorporated his parents' asceticism into his own life and theology, but he modified it by rejecting self-mortification, on one hand, and firmly accepting the fruits of assurance and the importance of thinking kindly but realistically of oneself, on the other. Ultimately, this ambivalence proved to be important.

His asceticism, combined with an emphasis on the fruits of assurance, structured his work. In 1731 in a letter to Mary Pendarves he related these elements to his underlying platonic metaphysical conviction that to imitate God is to become like God:

> I was made to be happy; to be happy I must love God. . . . To love God I must be like him, holy as he is holy; which implies both the being pure from vicious and foolish passions and the being confirmed in those virtues and rational affections which God comprises in the work of charity. . . . I lay it down as a rule that I can't be too happy or therefore holy.[10]

The mystic writers provided a model for his early desire to imitate God.[11] Following their reasoning, he believed that marriage was ontologically less perfect because of its sexual relationship. John Wesley's asceticism led him to view love relationships and marriage as a distraction in his single-minded pursuit of God. In "Thoughts on Marriage," he claimed:

> You were happy once; you know you were; happy in God, without being beholden to any creature. You did not need
> > Love's all-sufficient sea to raise
> > With drops of creature-happiness.
> . . . Is it not, in effect, loving the creature more than the Creator? Does it not imply that you are "a lover of pleasure more than a lover of God?"[12]

Under the criticism in the Annual Conference and by a correspondent that his thoughts were leading persons of weak judgment into "strange errors," he later modified his "Thoughts on Single Life and Marriage" to explicitly include marriage as a godly life, quoting Hebrews: "Marriage is honorable in all." Even so, Wesley continued to contradict himself in "Thoughts on a Single Life" when he defined liberty as "liberty from the flesh . . . from the greatest of all entanglements, loving one creature above all others." In "Thoughts on Marriage" he warned that men "should not seek in women what should be sought in God." Even so, he continued to prefer celibacy to marriage as an easier route to sanctification, teaching in the Annual Conference of 1745:

> Q.5. But would not one who was thus sanctified be incapable of worldly business? A. He would be far more capable of it than ever, as going through all without distraction. Q.6. Would he be capable of marriage? A. We cannot well judge. But supposing he were not, the number of those in that state is so small, it would produce no inconvenience.[13]

His objections to marriage were not only ontological; true to his platonism, he rejected marriage on instrumental grounds as well.[14] As Thor Hall pointed out, one rarely senses that Wesley valued his relationships intrinsically, for their own sake.

Wesley's initial rejection of marriage was based on a rejection of family responsibilities: children take up too much time and cost too much money.[15] At some points in his life he carried this opinion to shocking extremes. Regarding his decision to go to Georgia, he wrote, "But what shall we say to the loss of parents, brethren, sisters, nay, the friends of my own soul . . . if you add the loss of life to the rest, so much greater is the gain."[16] Writing to his sister, Martha Hall, upon the death of her three children, he "consoled" her:

> I believe the death of your children is a great instance of the goodness of God towards you. You have mentioned to me how much of your time they took up. Now that time is restored to you, and you have nothing to do but to serve our Lord without carefulness and without distraction, till you are sanctified in body, soul, and spirit.[17]

Evidently, John failed to notice that in spending time caring for her children, she was also "serving the Lord."

When John tried to persuade Charles that he should give his consent to John's marriage to Grace Murray, again John characterized his change of mind by an instrumental under-

124

standing of relationships. Although his rethinking moved him toward a relational model of communal rather than solitary self-sufficiency, he primarily attempted to win Charles' heart by arguing that Grace would be useful to him in his ministry. Charles should consent to the marriage because Grace was a good housekeeper, nurse, and Christian companion, and would not drain John's finances since he was already supporting her.[18]

Did Wesley's relational ethic allow him create a pattern of male-female relationships similar to those created under Neoplatonic self-sufficiency? During Wesley's most idealistically Neoplatonic phase, Wesley's relationships with women had remarkable similarities to those described by Elizabeth Clark in *Jerome, Chrysostom, and Friends*. Like Jerome and Chrysostom, Wesley developed "purely spiritual" relationships with several women whose Christian lives had merit in their own right. In these intimate, non-sexual relationships Wesley, like Jerome and Chrysostom, took on the male role of ethical and spiritual director in correspondence and in conversation even though his female friends were his "spiritual equal."[19] In fact, John's method of comforting his sister may have been a convention taken directly from the church fathers and mothers who also dealt with death of children by thanking God for "freeing them from a great burden."[20] Despite these relationships, he warned his followers against associating with women for fear that such contacts would stir up lust. When he wrote to Charles asking for advice about whether to marry Grace Murray, he subordinated Grace's ministry to his.

So far, the Wesleyan "alternative" regarding women and the family is no alternative at all. This sketch of his relational ethic, however, provides a backdrop against which to contrast the values of his economic ethic.

"The World Is My Parish": *Wesley's Economic Ethic*

In some respects Wesley's economic ethic is quite consistent with his Neoplatonic relational ethic.[21] Wealth seduces and corrupts; therefore, Wesley frequently reminded his hearers that to "make all you can, save all you can, give all you can" benefited their Christian character. Wesley, however, would not sanction the Christian's Neoplatonic escape from the life of necessity; nor would he entertain Aristotle's "natural" distinctions which create human and subhuman categories of people. With Luther, Wesley agreed that salvation is assured by God's prevenient, justifying, and sanctifying grace. Sanctification, or a life of good works, springs from faith. The sanctified life, Wesley insisted, is personal and social life which bears the scrutiny of God's justice. Unlike Luther, who through the common chest cared for the immediate community, Wesley refused to distinguish between the parishioner and the stranger. As a practical theologian, Wesley frequently used his observations of poor women to test the justice of personal and social economic practice.

Wesley called on his observations of poor women in order to highlight the division between the rich and the poor in Great Britain. "Thoughts on the Present Scarcity of Provisions," one of his most significant economic tracts, is a systematic reflection on the causes of poverty whose initial observations are fraught with female imagery:

> I ask, First, Why are thousands of people starving, perishing for want, in every part of the nation? The fact I know; I have seen it with my own eyes, in every corner of the land. I have known those who could only afford to eat a little coarse food once every other day. I have known one in London (and one that a few years before had all the conveniences of life) picking up from a dunghill stinking sprats, and carrying them home for herself and her children. I have known another gathering the bones which the dogs had left in the streets, and making broth of them, to prolong a wretched life! I have heard a third artlessly declare, "Indeed, I was very faint, and so weak I could hardly walk, until my dog, finding nothing at home, went out, and brought in a good sort of bone, which I took out of his mouth and made a pure dinner!" Such is the care at this day of multitudes of people, in a land flowing, as it were, with milk and honey! abounding with all the necessaries, the conveniences, the superfluities of life![22]

From this reflection Wesley described a chain of prey. The poor have no food because they are not employed. Workers are unemployed because the price of food has risen. Food prices are inflated because corn is used for distilling, which brings a higher price on the international market than bread; because oats feed the horses of the rich, rather than the common people; because dairy farms have become monopolized, driving up profits; because landlords habitually raise their rents. All of this serves the luxury of a few. The solution to the problem of "many thousand poor people starving? Find them work, and you will find them meat." Create jobs, reduce the national debt, reduce inflation, and abolish luxurious pensions to those who are alive. In other words, Wesley was convinced that the inequitable distribution of wealth, rather than scarcity, created poverty.

Similarly, Wesley criticized the poverty-producing policies of the colonies. Given his disinterested economic ethic, Wesley could not understand how the colonists could claim that they were enslaved to the British throne when they were building an economy based on African slave trade. In "A Calm Address to Our American Colonies" he challenged an American writer, saying:

> The writer asserts that he that is taxed without. . . .being represented is a slave. . . . I answer, No. . . . Who then is a slave? Look into America, and you may easily see. See that Negro, fainting under the load, bleeding under the lash! He is a slave. And is there 'no difference' between him and his master? Yes; the one is screaming, "Murder! slavery!" the other silently bleeds and dies!"[23]

In "Thoughts Upon Slavery" he began by describing the harmony of the Africans until the "Christians" arrived to enslave them. Arguing against those colonists who claimed that "furnishing us with slaves is necessary for the trade, wealth, and glory of our nation," Wesley countered, "wealth is not necessary to the glory of any nation; but wisdom, virtue, justice, mercy, generosity, public spirit, love of our country. These are the real glory of a nation; but abundance of wealth is not." Having kidnapped, herded, sold and inspected the slaves, the slavesellers divide the families:

> They are separated to the plantations of their several masters, to see each other no more. Here you may see mothers hanging over their daughters, bedewing their naked breasts with tears, and daughters clinging to their parents, till the whipper soon obliges them to part. . . . [They are] banished from their country, from their friends and relations forever, from every comfort of life, they are reduced to a state scarce anyway preferable to beasts of burden. . . . Did the Creator intend that the noblest creatures in the visible world should live such a life as this?[24]

He appealed for intervention into the slave trade at all levels of the economic system, demanding that procurers, merchants, and owners abandon their practice:

> Are you a man? Then you should have a human heart. . . . Is there no such principle as compassion there? Do you never feel another's pain? Have you no sympathy, no sense of human woe, no pity for the miserable? When you saw the flowing eyes, the heaving breasts, or the bleeding sides and tortured limbs of your fellow creatures, was you a stone, or a brute? Did you look on them with the eyes of a tiger? When you squeezed the agonizing creatures down in the ship, had you no relenting? Did not one tear drop from your eye, one sigh escape from your breast? . . . Regard not money! . . . Immediately quit that horrid trade: At all events, be an honest man.[25]

Wesley was seeking a conversion from a demonic economic practice, such as the one experienced by the slavetrader, John Newton, the "wretch" who upon his conversion wrote the lyrics of "Amazing Grace."

Wesley challenged specific economic policies, both in Great Britain and America. Theodore Jennings, in his recently published *Good News to the Poor: John Wesley's Evangelical Economics*, documents Wesley's complaints against the exploitive practices of merchants, distillers, doctors, lawyers. Doctors and lawyers line their own pockets by creating expensive practices, rather than providing adequate health care and legal advice to the poor. After summarizing Wesley's protest against the profit-motivated practices of doctors and lawyers, Jennings concludes: "When the commitment to the poor takes on the status of a normative claim, then what to others appears as the common and self-evident practice of merchants, doctors, and lawyers, appears instead as the practice of injustice and oppression."[26]

Wesley denounced national policies which encouraged war and colonialism, all the while underlining his belief that those nations who pursued policies which created poverty and suffering would be divinely judged. The want which was prevalent in America after the War for Independence, including the suffering of widows and orphans created by the war, was a signal of divine retribution against those who pursued the economic policies on which the country was founded.[27]

Wesley's attack on national policy did not allow individual Christians to abdicate their responsibility for one another, however. Albert Outler has neatly summarized Wesley's economic ethic this way:

> . . . has it ever struck you as odd that St. Paul and St. Karl agreed on the point of *greed* as the primal social sin? Wesley's rules were three: (1) social responsibility in the acquisition of property, capital or the means of production; (2) self-denial in one's stewardship of riches of every sort; and (3) the renunciation of all surplus accumulation. This Christian image of the Christian life was compounded by his rule of neighborliness: (1) my "conveniences" must give way to my neighbor's "necessaries"; (2) my "necessaries" must be shared with my neighbor's extremities (and "my neighbor" must be defined as anyone of God's other creatures whose need is anywhere within the range of my loving care—or yours).[28]

Furthermore, Wesley scrutinized practices of the care of the poor for the extent to which they misrepresented the poor or became self-fulfilling prophecies. On his visit to the Bedlam, the poorhouse, Wesley was impressed that the institutionalized poor were generally diligent people who became the victims of personal and social circumstance; however, the environment of the institution, the absence of friendship, education, comfortable shelter, and health care could not but create the personalities he encountered.[29] Wesley, unlike

Plato, was not afraid that Christians would become too compassionate; he used his highly descriptive writing to bring poverty and suffering close to those people who would otherwise live sheltered lives. In addition, as Jennings notes, Christian compassion began for Wesley with the face-to-face encounter, visiting the poor. It did not stop at charity, although "begging for the poor" was the next step to providing relief; Christian compassion found fulfillment in advocacy with the nations.[30]

Love of "Particular Creatures": Wesley's Domestic Economic Ethic

When Wesley talked about personal stewardship, or the way in which we are to use the economic resources that God has entrusted to us, his concept of stewardship included the necessity of providing for one's family. Whenever he appealed for donations for the poor,[31] he wrote: "Do you not know that God entrusted you with that money (All above what buys necessaries for your families) to feed the hungry, to clothe the naked, to help the stranger, the widow, the fatherless; indeed as far as it will go, to relieve the wants of all [hu]mankind?"[32] When people idolize their own families, as happens with a sector of society, the end of the formula must be emphasized. The parenthetical phrase is seemingly innocuous; so much so that Jennings, in an otherwise thorough summary of Wesley's economic ethic, makes no comment on it. Wesley's admonition to provide for one's family seems commonsensical and unnoteworthy until this admonition is considered in light of his experiences with his sisters.

Wesley would have liked to pattern his life after the scores of celibate religious who have shown that Christian generosity toward the neighbor is facilitated by a self-sufficient relational ethic.[33] Although he changed his mind about marriage, wrote an tract which amended his earlier "Thoughts on Marriage," and married, briefly and unhappily, Wesley increasingly had to struggle with the conflicts between caring for the parishioner and the stranger and caring for his family. Although he was initially idealistic about the celibate life described by the church fathers, Wesley did not get away with living an un-conflicted lifestyle of solitary self-sufficiency in his own life and disinterested economic generosity towards "the neighbor." He struggled to combine relational self-sufficiency, a disinterested economic ethic toward parishioners and strangers, and the love of "particular creatures" with the corresponding responsibilities for a family, a complicated and ambiguous matter.

Although "visiting the poor" was an essential experience in forming Wesley's economic ethic, Wesley's solitary self-sufficiency became inadequate in part because his impoverished sisters challenged both his bias and its implications. As a result, Wesley incorporated into his general economic ethic some values and principles which are important to public policies about women and family today.

The original Wesley family, as a clergy family, had status in the community, but after the Epworth parsonage fire they never emerged from indebtedness. The Wesley children, including the seven sisters, bore heavy emotional and economic responsibilities for their parents' poverty, according to the sisters' biographer, Frederick Maser. Only one sister, Anne, married well enough to escape poverty. John and Charles corresponded with his sisters Emilia Harper, Martha Hall, and Hetty Wright, about money and family obligations. Ultimately, each sister was widowed or deserted by her husband, and John and Charles provided her with financial support.[34]

The greatest theological challenge to Wesley's platonic self-sufficiency came from the vocal Emilia Harper. She differed with John about whether fixing on God alone meant rejecting the "worldly" happiness of human relationships:

> You seem to assert we ought to fix all our thoughts, hopes, and desires, on God alone . . . but sure that wise and good Being who formed us and gave us these bodies with their several desires and tendencies never designed to take away our liberty so far as to deny all subordinate love to the creature.[35]

In addition to challenging his theology, she claimed he was

creating his theology out of ulterior motives: he had lost the love of Sally Chapone.

After her husband deserted her, Wesley's sister Emilia was in increasingly poor health and financial straits. She appealed to John: "love to your sister in trouble is more pleasing to God than preaching to 1000."[36] In a later letter she pleaded for money, saying, "I am worse than a widow,"[37] alluding to the legal and economic protection which covered widows but not deserted wives. In a terse interchange between Emilia and John, she charged him to incorporate a personal economic ethic into his ethic of disinterested economic love for strangers and parishioners: "I impute all of your unkindness to me to one principle: that natural affection is a sin."[38] In reply John listed his most recent gifts to her and explained his own financial condition, retorting: "it is not whether natural affection is a sin, but whether it ought to supersede common justice."[39] He continued to provide her with financial support but chastised her for her lack of understanding and ungratefulness, calling her "the chief among sinners, whores and murderers not excepted."[40]

Ten years later Emilia still found it necessary to try one more time to convince her brother that he needed to theologically integrate his love of God and love of specific creatures. She wrote that she wanted to talk to him about his doctrines, "viz., no happiness can be found in any or all things in this world, *that*, as I have sixteen years of my own experience which lies flatly against it."[41] Her complaint was theological and economic. John claimed that she was ignoring the fact that he gave his own sisters more individual financial support than he gave to strangers.[42] A comparison of his record of his financial support of his sisters and his support of other families shows that his rebuff is accurate.[43]

Martha Hall and John Wesley carried on no such fiery correspondence, but Charles' and John's relationship to her life situation is revealing. Westley Hall had courted a younger sister Kezia, according to John, jilted her, and married Martha. When Samuel died, Susanna moved elsewhere, and Kezzy had nowhere to go except to the home of her brother Samuel (Jr.)

who agreed to house her if John would pay fifty pounds a year towards her expenses.[44] Kezzy went to live with Martha and Westley. After Westley became a Methodist preacher, he used his clerical and scriptural authority to seduce his female parishioners. Eventually, Martha tried repeatedly to leave Westley. She sought economic maintenance from him, but when it was not forthcoming, she returned to him until their final break in the mid-1740s. Over time, Martha cared for several of the women who became pregnant by Westley and for their children. Charles, mystified, asked how she could do such a thing. Martha, displaying her disinterested ethic of care, answered, "I knew I could obtain what I wanted from many; but she, poor hapless creature, could not, many thinking it meritorious to abandon her to the distress she brought upon herself. *Pity* is due to the wicked; the good claim *esteem*. Besides I did not act as a *woman* but as a Christian."[45] Regardless of where she placed the responsibility for the pregnancy, Martha Hall did not discriminate between "deserving" and "undeserving" women when it came to providing care.

Evidently, John and Charles were convinced by Martha's theology. Even though Westley Hall had renounced his association with the Methodists, John's reputation was maligned when rumors spread that he failed to discourage polygamy among his preachers. Despite these problems and regardless of John's cruel comfort at the death of her children, John and Charles provided long-term financial support, not only for Martha, but for Suky Hare and her son by Westley Hall, whom Martha had befriended. In this growing ethic of care Charles seemed to play a significant role and wrote to Martha, "look on my brother as the father of the family—for such he is, although I shall be glad to share the honor with him, without the name."

Martha's, John's, and Charles' ethics of care were strikingly different from that of their Puritan parents towards their sister Hetty. In the early 1720s Martha had fallen in love with a John Romley, but Samuel Wesley had forbidden their marriage. A few years later Romley seriously courted Hetty. Samuel again intervened. Eventually, Hetty, now in her late twenties, fell in love with a young lawyer, but Samuel still objected. Hetty eloped with the lawyer, spent the night with him, discovered that he did not intend to marry her, and returned the next day to her parents' house. She begged forgiveness and agreed to any marriage her father would arrange, fearing that she was pregnant. Her father arranged a marriage, but neither parent ever forgave her.[46] Although none of the siblings except Mary stood by Hetty at the time, John and Charles eventually decided that their unrelenting parents were too hard on Hetty. John wrote his sermon "On Charity" as a direct attempt to chastise his parents for their condemnation of Hetty.[47] Both of his parents recognized that they were rebuked by their son. Eventually, they made amends with John, but not with Hetty.

John's phrase, "all above what buys necessaries for your families" in the economic formula is not innocuous; rather, for us the admonition strikes at the heart of the problem of individual men who ignore or underpay divorce maintenance and child support and a society which often won't enforce its own court orders. What difference did these experiences make to development of the Wesleyan economic ethic? These personal experiences, combined with his visiting of the sick and imprisoned, convinced Wesley that the poor were human. Sometimes, the poor mismanaged funds, as his father had, but they "mismanaged" money far less maliciously than did those people who controlled economic power.

Wesley's multilayered concern for the poor, which calls individuals, families, and national policies to accountability, provides a necessary expansion of Luther's more domestic and ecclesial ethic. Together, Luther and Wesley create a voice within classical theology for shared responsibility on behalf of poor women and children. That voice, however, must be tested by the way in which women themselves have thought about the contributions and problems of mothering. To what extent is shared responsibility an American woman's tradition?

CHAPTER 6

Self-Sufficiency and Interdependence in American Women's Tradition

Motherliness will teach the mother how to remain at the
same time Madonna, the mother with her own child close
in her breast, and Caritas, as pictured in art: the mother who
at her full breast has room also for the lips of the orphaned
child.

Ellen Key[1]

Once we accept the theological idea of shared responsibility or interdependence as an ethic of care for poor women
and children, we are led to investigate ways that a multifaceted family policy might be constructed. A question, however, looms heavy on the horizon: Do women *want* a
comprehensive family policy? One of the reasons that such
policies as family allowances, parental leaves, child support
collection, child care, national health insurance, etc., have
traditionally received such little attention is that few large
groups of conservative or liberal women have lobbied for
them. Both liberals and conservatives fear that governmental
supports for families will reduce the autonomy of the family
to guide its own life. Many politically conservative women
have shied away from policies which give women economic
support apart from traditional family roles, arguing that such
role reorganization leads to a devaluing of the family. Many
feminists have relied on the political principle of the auton-

135

omy of the family in order to safeguard the right of family members to shape their lives in innovative ways, apart from what seems like the traditionally conservative influence of governmental policy. American women are politically diverse and agree on little, one might argue, but they seem to agree that they don't want a comprehensive family policy! The idea of shared responsibility represents a grand leap for women who cling to the idea of governmental non-intervention in the family.

The absence of support for family policy reflects some unique developments in American women's own tradition rather than a clear agreement that family policy cannot meet the needs of women and children at the present time. The strands of tradition within the American women's movement hold distinct and sometimes contradictory images of motherhood—but they also reveal its richness. These images—motherhood politicized, motherhood in conflict, motherhood idealized, motherhood professionalized, motherhood persevering, and one which was rejected, motherhood protected—are not "pure types" nor are they meant to be exhaustive of the possibilities for imaging motherhood. They do, however, represent distinct signposts which point toward ways that American women have understood mothering. They also reveal American women's own ethic of shared responsibility as their ethic of care.*

The Original Failure of Shared Responsibility

Early in the history of the United States the constitutional fathers sought to encode the enlightenment hope for individual civil equality into American law. Even though American

*I am using the colloquial term "American women's tradition" to refer to the public women's movement in the United States. Technically, a movement labelled "American" has a broader referent than the United States, and images within "women's traditions" would be far more inclusive than those within the public, largely white and middle-class women's movement. I wish to use the different images within the public movement to point toward that larger diversity.

tradition is filled with stories of the so-called "self-made man," early American thinkers assumed that the possibility of self-sufficiency depended upon the broader support of government and community. Early Americans had many ways of conceiving the relationship between the individual and the community, but even the most individualist of thinkers presupposed an ethic of care and interdependence which is very different than the ethic of self-sufficiency we are discussing today. Generally, they accepted the necessity of communal supports for the individual and led the early Americans to enact what was for them radical legislation which we now take for granted.

An example of their practical ethic of care is demonstrated in Thomas Jefferson's letter to James Madison in 1785. When he met a poor woman on the road in France, Thomas Jefferson, like Luther and Wesley before him, used her situation to test the viability of the new American laws. Jefferson's practical reflections reveal his recognition of the interdependence of the individual and the society in which she lives and his hope for a more equitable distribution of wealth in America than he witnessed in France.

At the time Jefferson was ambassador to France and observer of the French Revolution. His concern for the poor led him to write of the need for a relative economic equity which should grow from natural rights and social freedom. Jefferson's concern for freedom never sought freedom as an end in itself but sought freedom for the purpose of organizing a good society in which people could care for their families and communities. Freedom, as well as the natural right of property, served the pursuit of economic and relational justice. Freedom's promises were tempered by the continued presence of poor men, women and children in the community's midst. Jefferson's encounter points to his practical assumption that society exists for the care of all people.

After describing the town of Fountainebleau, a town of 15,000 which swelled to 20,000 each autumn when the king and his court came to hunt, Jefferson wrote of his walk to town:

> . . . I fell in with a poor woman walking at the same rate with myself and going the same course. Wishing to know the condition of the laboring poor I entered into conversation with her. . . . She told me she was a day laborer at 8 sous or 4d. sterling the day: that she had two children to maintain, and to pay a rent of 30 livres for her house (which would consume the hire of 75 days), that she often could get no employment and of course was without bread.[2]

Jefferson paid the woman 24 sous for guiding his trip, but he knew that his charity and her personal industriousness would not create her economic self-sufficiency. Rather, he was aware that her poverty was rooted in France's economic system:

> The property of this country is absolutely centered in a very few hands. . . . I asked myself what could be the reason so many should be permitted to beg who are willing to work, in a country where there is a very considerable proportion of uncultivated lands.[3]

The economic polarization of French society had created the luxury of the few and the poor woman's suffering. Reflecting on her situation, Jefferson recounted his belief in the right of all people to the property which enabled them to care for their families. The freedom to accumulate private property, for Jefferson, did not give a person the right to inordinate wealth but served one's right to feed, shelter, clothe and educate one's family. He realized that the problem of a poor woman's feeding her children required public, even "macroeconomic" solutions:

> . . . the consequences of this enormous inequality producing so much misery to the bulk of mankind [sic], legislators cannot invent too many devices for subdividing property. . . .
>
> The descent of property of every kind therefore to all the children or to all the brothers and sisters, or other relations in equal degree, is a politic measure and practicable one. Another means of silently lessening the inequality of property is to exempt from taxation below a certain point, and to tax the higher portions of property in geometrical progression as they rise. Whenever there are in any country uncultivated lands and unemployed poor, it is clear that the

laws of property have been so far exceeded as to violate a natural right.[4]

Jefferson thought that four radical and distinctively American changes in law would protect the United States from becoming a country in which a small percentage of the population owned the majority of wealth and property. These four changes formed "a system by which every fibre would be eradicated of antient or future aristocracy; and a foundation laid for a government truly republican." These changes would provide an effective barrier against an economically polarized society and would create the possibility of an equality of outcomes for children. The repeal of the law of entail, through which a family line gained the right to government and property, would prevent the economic sovereignty of an aristocratic family. The repeal of the law of primogeniture, which allowed families to consolidate their wealth in the hands of the oldest son, eliminated the poverty of his siblings by dividing inheritances equally among them. The restoration of the rights of conscience established religious freedom and eliminated the possibility that a rich, established religion could dominate poorer, dissenting sects. Finally, a radical and innovative entitlement program, public education, insured that people would have the basic knowledge which allowed them to understand their rights and to exercise self-government. The economic stability of the household, coupled with education, would enable children to become adults who could contribute to society.[5]

Revolutionary women, however, were less confident that these kinds of reforms would bring true equality to their lives. In her now-famous letter of March 31, 1776, Abigail Adams wrote to her husband, John:

> I long to hear that you have declared an independency—and by the way in the new Code of Laws which I suppose it will be necessary for you to make I desire you would Remember the Ladies, and be more generous and favourable to them than your ancestors. Do not put such unlimited power into the hands of the Husbands. Remember that all Men would be tyrants if they could. If particular care and attention is not paid to the Ladies we are determined to foment a

Rebellion, and will not hold ourselves bound by any Laws
in which we have no voice, or representation. . . .[6]

Women's hope for civil equality and economic equity was
dashed when they discovered that the new American principles did not apply to them. Abigail Adams predicted that until
men recognized that these principles must apply to all people,
women would not be satisfied. Her prophetic words were
fulfilled by a lively American women's tradition which itself
has developed many different emphases.

Motherhood Politicized

Through the practice of dissent which led to the Revolutionary War, American women were discovering their political lives. As in Great Britain John Wesley was attempting to
teach his followers to scrutinize their domestic economic
practices for the ways in which they exploited the poor,
American women were learning that their domestic lives had
taken on new, public meanings. The domestic became political as households organized boycotts against British products
and as Americans used homemade goods, such as clothing,
rather than buy from the British. In the years of the war,
women took over many formerly-male tasks on farms and in
businesses while their husbands went to war. When battles
landed on the women's property, they were expected to
make their homes into commissaries and hospitals. Women
were called on to declare their individual political allegiance,
decisions which had severe consequences for their marriages
and their right to retain or inherit property. As their domestic
lives became the foundation of the newly emerging public life
in America, women began to claim that women, as well as
propertied men, had natural, equal rights. This dawning hope,
Abigail wrote to John on May 7, 1776, was not made legally
explicit:

> I can not say that I think you very generous to the Ladies,
> for whilst you are proclaiming peace and good will to Men,
> Emancipating all Nations, you insist upon retaining an abso-
> lute power over Wives. But you must remember that Arbi-

trary power is like most other things which are very hard, vary liable to be broken, and notwithstanding all your wise Laws and Maxims we have it in our power not only to free ourselves but to subdue our Masters, and without violence throw both your natural and legal authority at our feet.[7]

Although women like Abigail Adams could not convince the constitutional framers to grant women full civil equality, women's imaginations synthesized their domestic lives and their emerging political consciousness. Women practiced this synthesis through a new image of mothering which Linda Kerber has called "Republican motherhood." Women who had practiced citizenship by scrutinizing their domestic activities for each political implication now educated their sons for good citizenship in the new republic. Only women educated in the ideals of the new republic could fulfill this responsibility well; therefore, educating women gained new importance. As well-educated women perpetuated the ideology of the natural equality, they also handed down its contradictions. In a country whose leaders proclaimed the philosophy of natural equality and inalienable rights, men practiced discrimination against the majority of the land's inhabitants. In homes where once their domestic activities had announced their political loyalties, women's lives became increasingly isolated and privatized. Unlike Wesley's unsuccessful attempt to teach his followers the socioeconomic meanings of their domestic habits, the contradictions of motherhood politicized did not go unnoticed by later generations of American women.

Motherhood Conflicted

The turn-of-the-century ideology of political domesticity, or "women's sphere," was challenged by the woman movement of the early 19th century. Not surprisingly, the struggles over motherhood and marriage among the inner circle of reformers reflect an image of motherhood conflicted in the ideology of the newly emerging woman movement.

The women in the inner circle of reformers led extremely different lives, as exemplified by Susan B. Anthony, Elizabeth

Cady Stanton, and Lucy Stone. As a child, Anthony had experienced the bankruptcy of her father's formerly-prosperous cotton mills. The resulting personal poverty was humiliating; until an uncle settled the debt, creditors threatened to sell all of the family's "unnecessary" possessions, including the children's underwear. In order to secure their livelihood, the daughters of the family had to marry or earn an income. As a result of this experience, Anthony, who never married, became a teacher to help to provide for the family. In her developing practical philosophy, Anthony applied the American tradition of self-reliance to women's financial hardships, advocating women's economic self-sufficiency. Recourse to marriage for economic security, she said, invariably led women into economic and psychological dependence on men which provided a false sense of security.[8]

Anthony's closest associate, Elizabeth Cady Stanton, launched the campaign for the natural rights of women through the Seneca Falls "Declaration of Sentiments," a revision of the Declaration of Independence which applied its principles to women. A talented writer and public speaker, Stanton was also a devoted mother of seven children. Her writings reveal that she cherished her children: "Imagine me . . . promenading the precious contents of a little crib"; they also record her desire for the freedom for public activity: "How much I do long to be free from housekeeping and children, so as to have some time to read, and think and write." She anticipated, however, that only a woman who had fully experienced "all the trials of women's lot" would truly be able to provide public criticism of the problems of "women's sphere."

The women around her, such as Anthony and Lucy Stone, were regretful of and somewhat impatient with her frequent retreat to domesticity; likewise, Anthony felt betrayed when single women within the movement, such as Stone, married at a late age and retired from public life. The women's passion for reformation and varieties of personal lifestyles produced situations in which they made temporary or permanent choices between "the cause" or domesticity, a choice between seeming opposites which was not unlike the one faced by the early monastic women.[9]

As they faced these personal choices, these women forged a practical philosophy which remained true to the universal themes which were lifted from the women's personal experience, even as the contours of the movement changed with 19th-century politics. As Stanton argued for women's right to speak publicly about abolition, she suggested that women had political lives beyond and apart from the sphere of politicized domesticity. Anthony added the idea that all women, including single and married women, must have legal and economic lives which are not merged with their husbands' legal and economic status. In reimaging womanhood, Stanton and Anthony suggested that the relation of men and women, even as co-parents, is based not on gender difference, but on the similarities in nature between women and men.[10] This shift helped the reformers recreate the rhetoric of natural rights into the language of "equal rights."

Based on the assumption of the equal rights of the sexes, Anthony and Stanton developed a criticism of the laws which regulated domestic life. Stanton argued that true marriage must be built not on laws and economic necessity but on "deep, fervent, love and sympathy." On this basis, Stanton advocated a series of domestic reforms: easier divorce laws so that women could leave destructive or violent marriages, an end to prostitution, abolition of the idea that wives and children are the "property" of husbands, women's control over frequency of sexual intercourse in marriage, and women's right to redress against the excess of violent or drunken husbands. When her critics charged that the principles of freedom and equality, applied to marriage, threatened the family, Stanton wrote:

> Here let me ask, how many truly harmonious households have we now? . . . The only happy households we now see are those in which husband and wife share equally in counsel and government. There can be no true dignity or independence where there is subordination to the absolute will of another, no happiness without freedom. Let us then have no fears that the movement will disturb what is seldom

found, a truly united and happy family. . . .[11]

The reformers had concentrated their efforts on the laws of the states; now, after abolition, they worked for civil and domestic reform through federal legislation. The Civil War had left widows and orphans, and Anthony hoped that increased economic opportunity for individual women would lead to women's economic self-sufficiency. Under the influence of late 19th-century capitalism, however, women's work became increasingly ill-paid and unfulfilling. Anthony attempted to merge her efforts on behalf of such goals as equal pay for equal work with trade unionism; however, her attempts met with only partial success.[12]

The domestic hardships of women as daughters and wives led to a necessary new philosophy of "the new true woman" who was not defined exclusively by the domestic sphere, a philosophy based on equal rights, economic and psychological self-reliance, and gender similarity. As the philosophy of the equal rights movement evolved, however, these groundbreaking premises led to some unfortunate conclusions. The romantic ideal of marriage also tended toward an elitism in parenting:

> . . . If law makers insist upon exercising their prerogative in some way on this question. . . . Let them fine a woman fifty dollars for every child she conceive by a Drunkard. Women have no right to saddle the state with idiots to be supported by the public. Only look at the statistics of the idiot asylums, nearly all the offspring of Drunkards. Women must be made to feel that the transmitting of immortal life is a most solemn responsible act and never should be allowed, except when the parents are in the highest condition of mind and body.[13]

Ironically, Stanton's reverence for life and children was tinged by her lack of realism regarding women who bear and raise children under less-than-ideal conditions. This irony was deepened by overt racism in the writings of Stanton and Anthony after the split in the suffrage movement between those wanted to argue for universal suffrage and those who felt that black male suffrage was most important.[14] For strategic and ideological reasons, the message of Stanton and Anthony failed to incorporate the explicit concerns of the poorest of women under the equal rights banner.

Motherhood Idealized

After the Civil War a variety of conditions gave rise to new trajectories in American culture which reflected a new image: motherhood idealized. The Civil War had left widows and orphans who now sought their own sustenance, and women's organizations arose to respond to their needs. The emancipation of slaves brought new challenges to those women who sought to promote the natural rights of women and blacks, resulting in a rift in the woman movement. The Reconstruction Era introduced the consolidation of capitalism, giving new urgency to the questions of labor and capital. Of particular significance to the shift in the image of mother, two movements which had been in their infancy before the war bloomed into full maturity: temperance and socialism. Within each of these movements, mother and home, as ideals for all of society, were central.

The antebellum woman's movement had been reminded of women's secondary political status when male abolitionists challenged women's right to an active, public role on behalf of abolition. This challenge resulted in the Seneca Falls Declaration of Sentiments of 1848. After the emancipation of slaves new conflicts arose over the best strategy toward suffrage for blacks and women. Lucy Stone and Henry Blackwell urged that black male suffrage, without the weighty encumbrance of universal suffrage, be prioritized; Stanton and Anthony argued that women's suffrage was as important, or more important, than black male suffrage. Unfortunately, after the suffrage movement split into organizations which pursued each goal, Stanton and Anthony occasionally argued that white women were "morally superior" and more deserving of the vote than black men. Although some of their language was explicitly racist, the rhetoric of moral superiority was consistent with the era's image of motherhood idealized.

The woman's suffrage movement was joined to the temperance movement through the organizational efforts of Frances Willard. Willard, a Wesleyan who grew up in German-Lutheran-dominated Wisconsin, brought the ideal of motherhood and home to public, political prominence. Willard understood "demon rum" as a menace to the home. Male sociability almost inevitably included gathering and drinking at the saloon, and alcohol turned gentle husbands and fathers into violent tyrants. When she organized the Women's Christian Temperance Union around the theme of "Home Protection," she argued that corporate and economic interests of the saloon keepers, rather than the sanctity of home, were being protected by government. In doing so, she challenged the simplistic idea that alcoholism was an individual moral sin and that abstinence was a personal piety; rather, she organized women around the notion of the saloon as a economic institution, which, with political support of government, wreaked havoc in families. The alcohol industry, with the saloon as its local institution of male education and initiation, seduced young boys and destroyed the lives of women and children through debt and violence. If the saloon, in reality and metaphorically, became the image of destruction which represented American social organization at its worst, the image of salvation was "motherhood" and "home." With full political rights through suffrage, women could rout the evil of alcohol from society and "make all the world homelike."

Willard popularized the idea of the good society as "home" and the good individual as "mother-hearted" women and men. "Mother-hearts" are not biological parents but men and women who exhibit the generosity of neighbor-love, people who care not only for their own families and children but for all of the world's children. Men can be mother-hearts as well as women; in fact, tender fatherliness becomes "a new and, perhaps, more prophetic role":

> Motherhood will not be less, but fatherhood a hundred-fold more magnified. . . . For when to the splendor of their intellectual powers and the magnificence of their courage shall be added the unselfish devotion that comes of

"childward care," we shall see characters more Christ-like than the world has known save in its calendar of saints.[15]

In their "coming beatitude," men would be raised to the moral superiority of women, rather than women degraded by the moral laxity of the world of men.
Although her prime example of a mother-hearted woman was Susan B. Anthony, Willard imagined continuity, rather than conflict, between the personal home and the home of the society. Home, for Willard, was "man and woman added to a house," "a mirror repeating their united thought, sentiment, purpose and taste," "a place conscious of wise benignant personality; instinct with lives that are noble and beloved; differentiated as thoroughly from other homes as its founders are dissimilar in character, education and inmost intent from other people."[16] Home was a humanizer, a breeding place of character and virtue, a refuge, an anchor.

Unlike many romantic images of home, in which a gentle and protected woman waits to comfort a man brutalized by the world, Willard's homeyness was gender-equal, a human quality based on a legal and economic status attainable by women as well as men. Just as men took on the wisdom and kindness of home, women were no longer relegated to legal or economic submission in marriage. Rather than emphasizing the need for divorce as justice for unhappy families, as did Stanton, Willard envisioned marriage as a life-long commitment based on a partnership of equals. This equality would be established through

> . . . coeducation to mate them on the plane of mind, equal property rights to make her God's own free woman, nor coerced into marriage for the sake of a support, not a bondslave after she is married, who asks her master for the price of a paper of pins and gives him back the change. . . .[17]

This image of homeyness and equality, love and justice, envisioned the success of life-long, monogamous marriage due to the desirability of marriage rather than the coercion of law. By analogy, for Willard, an attitude of love which fulfills female and male expressions of gender, supported by a framework of gender justice, became a political metaphor for society. Transformed by mother-heartedness, society would breed virtue, rather than vice; offer affection, comfort and kindliness, rather than hostility and coldness; provide care and cooperation, rather than ruthless competition. An equal legal and economic relationship between the genders would assure that mother-heartedness could be offered freely, without exploitation.

Willard was far more optimistic about the possibilities of happy families than Anthony, probably because her home of origin exemplified the ideals she envisioned for society. She recognized, however, that families and society were often not presided over by mother-hearts, a realization which grounded her political organization of the W.C.T.U. and her support of service groups which befriended intemperate and abandoned women and destitute children.[18] The concept of mother-heartedness, or mother-breastedness, provided a cultural metaphor for the full-scale practice of social work in the settlement house movement by such reformers as Jane Addams, mother of social work and founder of Hull House in Chicago.[19]

Meanwhile, in a tradition brought to the United States by German-American immigrants as early as 1848, the protection of home and the joy of domesticity were emphasized and debated among spokespersons for the growing American socialist movement. Exhibiting "a reverence for women and devotion to family life," early socialists believed in separate gender spheres for the proletarian family, in which men earned a family wage and women protected "depth of sentiment, warmth of heart, and strength of feeling." Women in America sought equal rights because their families were devoid of this joy, one immigrant socialist remarked. The early socialists collapsed the problem of gender into class, teaching that the "woman problem" would be resolved through class warfare, after which a woman "would retreat from the workaday world, resist the appeal of individualism inherent in the women's rights campaign, and regain her 'natural' relationship with man at the hearth, realizing herself in the family life now impossible under capitalism."[20] Women's life within socialism was organized by pre-political social organizations which reflected the ethnic celebrations, rituals, and community life of the old world.

Women within the socialist movement, however, began to argue that theoreticians' understanding of the relationship between women and socialism was misconceived. In the 1870s free-thinkers, such as Augusta Lilienthal, called into question the socialists' aversion to women's labor, arguing that a woman who needed to win bread for her family should be supported, rather than rendered destitute and helpless by socialist prejudice against women's labor. Urging the socialists to reconsider the claims for citizenship among women of the equal rights movement, she argued that women, like the proletariat, were stateless. The problem with the women's rights movement was not that it was antagonistic to socialism but that it did not go far enough in arguing for women's economic equality. The *Frauenbund*, the women's organization within socialism, began to push for economic reforms which supported the family: equal pay for equal work, shorter workdays, and labor protection for children. In the 1890s Joanna Greie forwarded a critique of socialist marriage which envisioned "the shared comradeship of man and woman [which] would foreshadow the new society within the old."[21]

Although they proceeded from different beginning points, the similarity between images of domesticity, equality of men and women, and economic reforms in the workplace led to collaboration of reform-minded Christians such as Willard and Addams and turn-of-the-century socialists. In what became known as Christian socialism, reformers fought for domestic love, marital equality, and civil and economic reform for poor men, women, and children, until the Bolshevik Revolution and World War I dashed the reformers' hopes for a socialist reign of God on earth.

Motherhood Professionalized

The tradition of the early 20th-century feminist movement merged concerns for women's economic opportunities, suffrage, and women's psychosexual well-being. On the heels of the socialist fight for women's economic rights, but deeply influenced by the emerging discussions of sexuality as exemplified by Freudian psychology, women in America for the first time claimed themselves as psychosexual beings whose sexual expression could be affirmed and publicly discussed. Although a variety of topics concerning women's economic opportunities revolved around the relationship between employment and sex, no analysis relating sexuality, employment, and mothering appeared in the American movement.[22]

Several attitudes towards women's labor were evident after the turn of the century. Women were entering the labor market in most professional fields. The spokeswomen for the National Women's Party argued that women's equality could be best achieved by continuing to increase women's economic opportunities. Wage-earning would provide women with economic independence and would challenge the sexual division of labor in the home.

Women initially suggested different ways to combine a career, marriage and motherhood. As the psychological sciences gained prominence, women entered professions which were logical extensions of mothering, such as research in early childhood development. Some women, however, became educated and employed in male-dominated professions and began to suggest ways that women could combine career, marriage and motherhood. Generally, women needed extensive psychological and economic support, such as supportive husbands and paid domestic help, to manage the stress of the three jobs. Some women recognized that women could not be left to their individual devices to coordinate three such demanding tasks. According to the Howes Institute for Coordination of Women's Interests at Smith College, only "transforming the whole social setting and inner attitudes of men and women" would make the combination possible. The combination might also be possible if women recognized homemaking as a "career." Marriage and motherhood might not be something which came by women naturally, the newly organized professionals in home economics suggested; homemaking and mothering were skills in which women should be trained. Under this rubric, motherhood for the first time came to be considered a "profession in the home."

Encouraged by the rise of the social sciences, women also began to reflect on their own sexuality. Unlike the late 19th-century economic reformers who linked social service and chastity, some 20th-century women, such as the members of Heterodoxy, began to believe that economic and sexual independence for women could lead to a transformation of women's own self-understanding and the relation between the sexes. Women who began to experiment with sexual freedom outside of marriage began to erase some of the boundaries between "pure" and "fallen" women. Women who explored their sexuality within a monogamous relationship, whether or not it was legally sanctioned, suggested that women's economic and sexual freedom would enhance relational satisfaction since women and men could enter truly desirable relationships. Although American women speculated about the influence of sexual and economic freedom on marriage, they never attempted to argue that mothering could be compatible with this lifestyle. Knowing that these ideas were politically volatile, they avoided linking sexual and economic freedom with the civil freedom they sought in the suffrage movement.[23]

Those persons representing the interests of working-class women, however, were not convinced of the emancipatory effect of sexual liberation, suffrage, and employment. According to the Women's Bureau, labor protection for women rather than individual economic opportunity would emancipate women from their true drudgery: overwork. Arguing that most women worked because of economic necessity rather than for economic fulfillment, the Women's Bureau described the disintegration of family and childhood which was caused by the exploitation of women in labor: long hours away from home for mothers and children, poor pay, and unhealthy conditions. The Women's Party argued that women wanted to work for their self-fulfillment, but the Women's Bureau countered that most women's labor was degrading and exploitive. Women's labor deprived many mothers and their children of adequate economic and emotional sustenance.

Motherhood Persevering

The first four images of motherhood represent distinct, historically-recorded moments in the American women's movement. Beside these actively debated self-understandings of women lies a quiet but no less tenacious image: motherhood persevering. The unnamed women who are recorded in men's writings, such as those anonymous women memorialized by Augustine, Luther, Wesley, and Jefferson, left little written or spoken record of their self-understanding. Their tenacity, however, matches the enduring quality of the fragments of the images which eventually reemerge, even though they have been ignored by the systematizers and experts. These women have frequently offered their children an image of humanness so full—so fraught with the extremes of anguish, sorrow, impertinence, delight, and diligence—that it shocks and sobers those mothers who live more sheltered, comfortable and privileged lives.

Although mothers of all races and ethnicities have persevered in their goal of providing life for a new generation, black women have been particularly vocal about their respect for the wisdom of their mothers as spiritual and practical guides. Cicely Tyson describes the sentiments of many black women when she writes:

> Role model? My mother leads the pack. When I think of the price she paid for "this life," I regard her as I do all of the other black women through history: miraculous. They are miracles in this human race. Somehow they are always at the bottom of the ladder, the last rung. Yet despite the pain, the bruises, and the bleeding, they did not let go. They hung on for as long as they could and when they felt they had rallied enough strength from within to reach the next rung, they did. Those are the role models![24]

In the black church tradition a particular women's role as the wise mother is frequently recognized throughout the church and community. Known as "church mothers," these women become the comforters, organizers, and guides of younger women and men. The sense of egalitarian caring epitomizes the church mothers. In the words of one, "I am always fearful of mistreating strangers because I know no matter who the man or woman might be that he is some mother's son, and she is some mother's daughter, and I really believe God wants us to truly love everybody."[25] As black women have developed a public, womanist tradition, they have drawn on the moral wisdom of the older generations of black mothers, as recognized by Katie G. Cannon in *Black Womanist Ethics*:

> Black woman's collection of moral counsel is implicitly passed on and received from one generation of Black women to the next. Black females are taught what is to be endured and how to endure the harsh, cruel, inhumane exigencies of life. . . . The moral counsel of Black women captures the ethical qualities of what is real and what is of value to women in the Black world.[26]

The writing of black women suggests their deep respect for the wisdom of their collective mothers.

Motherhood Protected

A tradition which did not take hold among women in the United States is represented by the figure Ellen Key, a Swedish feminist of the turn of the century who laid the philosophical groundwork for family policy. As a Scandinavian, Key was one of the first women to use the term "feminism," but she did not hearken to American women's concern for equal rights.[27] Instead, she argued that the conditions of women's flourishing included and superseded women civic equality: women's equal rights included a right to mother. Unflustered by the anonymity of the lost generations of nameless women, she credited them with the grand accomplishment of transmitting cultural heritage through their mothering.[28] In words reminiscent of those 19th-century women who had argued for the moral superiority of women, Key argued the repression of female nature and the suppression of the desire to mother was women's primary problem. Key, however, is a woman more representative of the 20th century than of the 19th. Analogous to Luther in his assertion that the faithful love of two people, rather than the law, created a marriage in God's sight, Key held fast to the belief that soulful love, rather than the law, created genuine human partnership.[29] This love, within or apart from legal marriage, offered the best context for the creation of children. In so arguing, Key appealed to the emerging feminists who wanted to articulate their psychosexual experience.

Like Luther, who linked the ideas of sexuality and parenthood, Key joined the two concepts to urge women's growth in this psychosexuality and the expression of this sexuality in mothering. In a reversal of what I have called politicized domesticity, which brought the home into the public sphere, Key called on the state to expand protective labor legislation for women to include reproductive labor. If the state protected motherhood through its social policies, romantic love, rather than the coercions of economics and law, could provide the basis for marriage. Key successfully argued for political policies which protected motherhood, and Scandinavian family policy was born.[30] Key's turn-of-the-century ideals about marriage and the family predicted in an uncanny way the direction that family patterns in the United States have actually developed—but without state support for mothering. Since Key emphasized the importance of sexuality, she was rejected by the late 19th-century U.S. woman movement; since she rejected the emphasis on civil and personal economic rights in favor of state-supported mothering, she was rejected by the 20th-century feminist movement.

Women's Understanding of Shared Responsibility

These snapshots of American women's tradition create a collage of the ways that domesticity and mothering have been practiced, reflected upon, and valued in the United States.

These images reflect the deep wisdom of American women—not as individuals, from whom one can gather many different opinions about domesticity and motherhood, but as a tradition—and reveal a portion of the American woman's legacy. Women have shared the responsibility not only for children and families but also for the shape of the communities and nation in which they lived. Women have cared for others through domestic tasks which offered women's tenderness, comfort, and courage. The costs borne by some women, such as domestic servants who were drawn from their own homes in which they were needed and wives who were isolated in homes where their social contributions were constrained, created deep suffering for them and their loved ones. Some women, such as Stanton, felt the constant pull of private and public life; other women, such as Anthony and Key, cared for the children of their sisters. Women such as Willard and Addams developed institutions and agencies through which persevering mothers and children could be offered the physical care, comfort, guidance, and stability of the home life they did not have. All of these women, in their different emphases of care, found it impossible to separate the individual and social, private and public aspects of care for one another. For them, the idea of shared responsibility for poor women and children, through personal practice and through the shaping of culture and society, is not argued so much as assumed.

Since Revolutionary days the common wisdom of American women has recognized that domesticity is not a sheltered, privatized matter; rather, domestic practice could shape the politics of the nation. Domestic practice, however, has not been the only lever in women's self-determination. The civil principle of equality offered a unique opportunity for women to make formal claims for their equality with men. These formal claims have led to conflicts among mothers since such claims have created opportunities and obligations for women while necessarily ignoring the varieties of ways that women have made unique contributions to America's moral life. At times, American women have held the nation accountable for fulfilling its egalitarian promise by claiming women's rights, but at other times, American women have also sparked the nation's conscience by insisting that the vulnerable among us must be protected and cared for. In these ways American women have forged their own understanding of shared responsibility.

The conscience of American women, however, has become entangled in a series of questions which remain unresolved in American women's traditions. In today's socioeconomic conditions, women's commitments to equality and care may not be realized through the means women have traditionally employed.

The first question regards women's relation to the state. If women claim the right to civil and economic equality, must women then relinquish the right to special state support for maternity and mothering? Or if women emphasize the need for special support for mothering, must they then relinquish their claim to full civil and economic equality? If women accept state support, does that diminish their right to make autonomous decisions?

The second question regards women's relation to the economy. Women are engaged in both productive and reproductive labor. If women emphasize the economic value of their productive labor, including the right to secure the opportunities of the marketplace and to be paid an equal wage for their work, do they then negate women's reproductive and domestic labor whose benefit is not easily measurable in economic terms? If women emphasize their contributions to the quality of life in the home, do they then diminish their claim to full economic rights?

The third question concerns women's roles within the family and women's rights to be autonomous individuals. If women value the connectedness of the family, do they then diminish their right to autonomous expression, including their individual right to make autonomous decisions concerning sexuality and the use of their bodies? If women exercise their autonomy, do they threaten to weaken the family?

The fourth question concerns the pluralism of women's experience. If women organize for power in society, must they truncate their concerns, excluding the concerns of some women? If women attend to the concerns of women who come from a variety of experiences, will their ability to wield power be diluted by the internal battles about which women's experience is privileged? How can women promote policies which do not discriminate among married mothers, single mothers, and women who are childless, among white women and women of color, among women whose traditions arise from different class backgrounds? What political strategies will not pit women against women?

Historically, American women have dealt with these questions by creating different trajectories of tradition which responded to various aspects of women's conditions. The women's voice and the classic theological traditions are formed around a similar goal: human flourishing. The classic theologians would urge American women to evaluate their own traditions by the criterion with which women frequently judge theology and policy: care of the vulnerable. Women's practices—of politicizing domesticity, of claiming women's civil and economic rights, of protecting women and children's labor, of encouraging women's control over their sexuality, of highlighting contributions to culture of scores of nameless mothers, of recognizing that mothering is not guided exclusively by an instinct available to all women but also by women's practical reason and skill—all represent partial contributions to the process of caring for vulnerable women and children. The theological criterion of care of the vulnerable reminds women to look for the accomplishments of each of these, and other, women's practices, rather than relying upon any one solution.

CHAPTER 7

Shared Responsibility

I want you to take Hillary. I want you to find her a home.
. . . We stay in places where you are afraid to fall asleep. We
eat food nobody else wants. We spend all day on the street,
walkin' with no place to go. People look at us like we're
trash. . . . It's the loneliest kind of life. It's no way for a child
to live. Maybe others can give her better. . . . We've always
been poor, Mr. Reed. My mother, my grandmother, and her
mother before that. We worked hard and we sweated but
we ain't never been anything but poor. I don't know how
to stop that for Hillary. I don't know how. Except give her
to somebody else. . . . It's the best thing I can do, isn't it?
Maybe she'll grow up to be healthy, and strong. And maybe,
someday, she'll forgive me for what I done. I love my
daughter, I love my daughter. I love her so much.

Theresa Johnson[1]

Women's Changing Roles

In the 1880s their son returned from the United States
with glowing reports, and Anna and Franz were convinced.
The United States *was* the land of opportunity, and the fertile
farmlands of Ohio could provide a sustenance for the entire
family. Gathering all of their sons and daughters and their
husbands and wives, Anna and Franz traveled by ship and train
from Switzerland to Ohio. Their stern, German-Swiss determi-
nation served them well, and they populated and cultivated a
large portion of farmland just south of Lake Erie. Their daugh-

ter, Rosetta, and her husband, Albert, farmed and bore eight children, among whom one of the youngest was Louise. Louise met and married an aspiring ore freighter mate, Pete. Known for his good judgment and safety, Pete shortly became a captain. While Pete sailed the lake, Louise farmed, supported Roosevelt, kept the family financial records, and cared for their son, their farmhands, and various relatives. She entertained them by writing songs, music and lyrics, singing around the piano, collecting coins and stamps, and keeping the family vegetable stand stocked.

Barbara and Elizabeth, who were young women at the turn of the century, travelled alone from Hungary to Newark, seeking work. Barbara found employment as a domestic servant, married another Hungarian immigrant, and bore three daughters, whom she continued to support by cleaning houses. Elizabeth became a soda jerk, married William, an English bricklayer whose language she barely knew, and bore five sons and a daughter. When William died, her thirteen-year-old son, Bill, apprenticed to an electrician. He helped to support his mother, brothers, and sisters until his mother remarried and his siblings could find employment in the Garfield mills. Through the mills he met Barbara's oldest daughter, Paula, a bookkeeper and secretary. After Paula and Bill married, Paula rejoiced at the thought of settling at home to raise two daughters. When the Depression struck, she salvaged their new home by renting it and moving to a small apartment in a building she managed. She eventually acquired several apartment buildings while Bill became a foreman in the electrical trades. They cared for the children first, being sure that the children wanted for nothing, even when the adults were in need.

Paula's daughter, Barbara, the first woman of the family to attend college, studied in Ohio and met and married Louise's son, Jim. Barbara, a mother of the fifties, raised a daughter and a son and volunteered in service clubs and church, while Jim helped his parents develop a newly-formed shipping business. Louise taught the daughter to spell and to read the stock pages, discouraged her aspirations to become an actress, but conceded that her desire to become a stewardess on an airplane was a more realistic goal. In the seventies the business declined and Barbara completed college, Barbara and Jim divorced, and Barbara worked in social service. Their daughter completed college, settled down to married life with an aspiring corporate manager, bore two more daughters, went back to graduate school, divorced, and began a professional life as a single parent. Paula and her sister Len, watching in bewilderment as their daughters and granddaughters reentered the work force, commented to one another, "But we were so happy when we could stay at home!"

The ideals and realities of women's work and family lives have changed dramatically with each generation. As the great-great-granddaughters of Rosetta, Barbara, and Elizabeth enter young adulthood, what kind of women's world has been prepared for them?

The Irony of Realism in Young Women's Worlds

The world of young women is continuous with the world of their foremothers in that these women must be prepared to combine nurturing and providing. Unlike their ancestors, however, they take it for granted that they will have as many opportunities for providing as men do, and that their husbands, if they have husbands, will share in caring for children. As women, they expect themselves to be equal inheritors of the American Dream in a way unlike any previous generation of women.

Ruth Sidel's study of young women aged 12–25 suggests that young women, regardless of race or class, believe in self-sufficiency as the means to a happy end: a fulfilling job, happy mothering (with or without a co-parent), and an economically secure—even affluent—lifestyle. By studying their expectations Sidel distinguished three versions of the self-sufficient ideal. One group of young women, whom she called the New American Dreamers, believe that individual "success is there for the taking; all they need to do is to figure out the right pathway and to work hard. Above all, they believe they must be prepared to go it alone."[2] The second group, the Neotraditionalists, have a stronger, but by no means exclusive, commitment to family as a center in their lives. The third group, the Outsiders, perceive themselves as so far beyond the mainstream of society that they cannot imagine a way to negotiate their way into its opportunities. They act out their disappointment by committing suicide or becoming involved in drugs, alcohol, or crime.

Sidel notes perceptively that all adolescents, for a time, become "outsiders" in that they reject adult values in order to secure their own. The goal of young adulthood, however, is to reenter society ready to take an adult role. Today's young women may be unprepared for sustaining that reentry because they share such unrealistic expectations of the roles they will enter. They expect to find work which pays better than most "women's work." They still seek long-term, committed, intimate relationships which are becoming increasingly rare. Many of them still want children but have few plans for adequately caring for these children. Sidel's record of the contradictions in young women's expectations leaves the definite impression that these young women cannot see the obstacles they face.

This seeming lack of realism about society's limits points toward the shadow side of the experience of a generation who were children during the last two decades of cultural upheaval—a side which, I suggest, is ironically realistic. Having lived through periods of great instability in many of their own families and in culture generally, these young women are *depending upon* being able to go it alone. Intuiting that they cannot trust the support upon which previous generations relied, many young women cannot allow themselves to admit that they might not be able to be self-sufficient. They cannot *afford* to acknowledge the extent to which family connections, communities bound by ethnicity and race, and social supports have anchored those persons who were touted as self-sufficient in the past. Otherwise, they would be forced to face—as did some of their mothers and grandmothers—the terrifying vulnerability of "going it alone."

Whether or not they will be required to reenact the experiences of some past generations of women and children who have struggled alone will depend upon, in part, whether mature generations of men and women can learn from women's experiences. Have we learned the lessons that generations of mothers, beginning with Abigail Adams, have tried to teach? These lessons teach us that deceptive illusions of equality are produced when women declare themselves equal without restructuring workplace policies, or when one woman gains pay or position equal to her many male peers but women's labors and insights are generally devalued or romanticized, or when many women spend their lives caring and providing but die lonely or early. Can mature women *afford* to study those lessons, the lessons which teach us that what we hoped were destinations in the journey toward equality are signposts pointing toward the next road? For if we do, we come face-to-face with the kinds of legacies and disenfranchisements that we will offer to the next generation of women. We will discover that if we deny the invisible lines of support which create their equality, our privileged daughters may continue to inherit their share of Plato's self-sufficiency, while our less privileged daughters remain invisible. If we concede that the fight for "equality" has been a deceptive ruse, we leave all our daughters a share in Aristotle's option of subordination by economic necessity. But if we are willing to pay the price, our theological commitments will motivate us to offer our daughters a vehicle and a map toward a new destination: toward interdependence, shared responsibility, and an ethic of care.

Theology and Public Policy

On what basis can we establish a dialogue between theology and public policy? When Jefferson wrote to Madison from France, he affirmed his belief that the separation of church and state would prevent a new religious aristocracy from developing. Since that time, Americans have regarded the principle of the separation of church and state as a mainstay of procedural justice. The American founders, however, would rarely have argued that religious conviction is somehow separate from the people's motivations or rhetoric about public policy. In contrast, since the technological revolutions of the late 19th and early 20th centuries, Americans had come to believe that science was "value-free"—the implication being that not only our procedures but also our motivations and beliefs could and should be separated from the forming of public policy. This position has now come under suspicion, both by persons in the social-scientific world who recognize that religious values infuse scientific methods, data, and interpretations, and by persons in the religious world who have argued that Americans disguise their religious commitments in their unarticulated civil religions.

In this work I have attempted to restore the dialogue between our religious and civil motivations and rhetoric by creating a collage of women and children from the theological history and women's tradition. These traditions of shared responsibility create a mirror, a reflection of a vision of social and interpersonal relationships in which basic support is provided to all. When we hold up the vision of our present social and interpersonal practices in the same mirror, we are struck by the radical disjuncture of the images we see. The radical non-identity of our theological commitments and our present practices cause us to reject practices based on a norm of self-sufficiency.

The Problem with Self-Sufficiency

Self-sufficiency is fundamentally determined by detachment of persons from one another, both relationally and economically. It holds individuals so fully responsible for their own lives that they cannot be moral agents without giving up relational and economic power. When this renunciation is the route to the imitation of the divine, there is no room for the moral agency of parents and society on behalf of children; there is no protection of the most vulnerable.

Welfare reform and divorce reform laws which are built on models of self-sufficiency echo many of the same themes. When public policy makers uphold a model of psychological and economic self-sufficiency as the goal of interpersonal and social existence, that model denies the reality of the fundamental supports of most "self-supporting" people and ignores the importance of all people's social contribution and participation. Self-sufficiency devalues parenting and creates a perversion in gender relations. Since mothers are traditionally responsible for children, single mothers have been socially valued when they work "double shifts" as they attempt to support their children economically and psychologically. Fathers are socially valued when they become "successful" in the pursuit of their own goals, even when they fail to maintain relationships with their children. In contrast, when we recognize the interdependence of the domestic and public worlds, we will provide basic care for all while encouraging each person's social contribution.

Self-sufficiency also normalizes perverse race and class relations. In Greek thought, those who are not self-sufficient, who provide basic support services for those who are deemed self-sufficient, are designated subhuman. Traditionally, Americans regarded blacks and women as legally subhuman (black males were valued at 3/5 of a free white male and women had no value except in relation to men). Despite our present legal valuing of each person, the tradition of self-sufficiency reflects the Greek and American traditions of subhuman designation. Under our present norm of self-sufficiency, those persons who live in communities which have few stabilizing social institutions, underfunded public schools, decreased interpersonal job networks, and fewer opportunities for employment which can support a family, are held as morally responsible for their "self-sufficiency" as those who live in communities with stable institutions, well-resourced public schools, and high-paying employment opportunities. These communities are disproportionately composed of people of color. Despite these structural disadvantages, our welfare reform practices, such as workfare, reinforce the idea that persons in these communities have an "equal" chance at self-sufficiency. When they do not attain economic self-sufficiency, their personal lack of moral responsibility, not society's devaluing of domestic work or the impact of impersonal macroeconomic trends, becomes the problem. In other words, the norms of self-sufficiency, even today, devalue those people who live "the life of necessity."

Shared Responsibility: A Theological Framework

This study of medieval practices, Luther, Wesley, and American women provides a framework for creating a theological voice in the dialogue over U.S. domestic family policy. This voice asks three fundamental questions: What is the quality of the divine-human relationship? How do we conceive of the human within this relationship? How do we exercise the care of the neighbor as taught by the Great Commandment?

The idea that God first extends God's grace toward humankind shocks human beings into complacency. God's first offering God's grace to humanity is such a radical idea that we are tempted to believe that God, and especially the theologians, didn't really mean it. Yet Augustine, Luther, and Wesley all agree with this basic idea. If God is active in human life before humans are aware of it, human expectations of one another are turned upside-down. Since these theologians proclaimed this idea when the church did not, they were denounced, mobbed and stoned. The gospel of God's grace is upsetting to the philosophy of self-sufficiency because it makes God's benefits available to all, without choosing its recipients on the basis of the "natural distinctions" of gender, race, or class.

The recognition of God's grace leads us into a fundamental ethic of care. Although the tradition of self-sufficiency created pressure from within the tradition for Christians to detach themselves from the world, they were called back into the world by Christ's invitation to serve their neighbors. The medieval compromises represented ways in which church theology responded to the practical needs of the people. Rather than applying formal norms regardless of practical realities, these compromises recognized the vision of care as well as the imprecision and the vulnerability which infuses everyday life. They represent common practices which are barely fathomable within the modern mindset until we recognize them as practices of care which arose at the intersection in that era of belief, rhetoric, and care. The study of these practices urge us to ask: What kinds of practices of care might represent the modern compromises which do the same in contemporary society?

Luther focuses on the delight of domesticity and care of the neighbor as the practice of the love of God; Wesley emphasizes that the care of God's creation is a fundamental responsibility of stewardship. In Wesley's words, all people must have the "necessaries of life" before a few have life's luxuries. If people are without life's necessities, Christians are not to justify the situation by labeling the poor undeserving. Wealthy Christians (in Wesley's terms, those with the basic necessities of life and anything left over) are to examine their own practices and the practices of the communities in which they participate, in order to ensure that they are providing for their neighbor in need. When Wesley's economic policy failed, it left a void which the policy of the economic survival of the fittest rushed to fill.

In need. What do human beings need? Luther provides the fullest interpretation of human need which is incorporated into his understanding of domesticity. Basic human need includes economic support, physical care such as food, shelter, clothes, health care, and for Luther, sex. Luther bases his idea of domesticity in his interpretation of biological needs, but biological needs serve relational purposes: affection, companionship, and the care of the vulnerable, including children and poor neighbors. In its fundamental concepts, domesticity is not an enclosed system, nor an isolated, protected haven from a heartless world, but a part of the ecology of human vocation in all of life. As the Lutheran perspective gained hold, however, it contributed to the breakdown of this ecology by privatizing women. When this ecology breaks down due to the coercive effect of larger institutional practices, those practices are deemed exploitive and must be reviewed.

This ecology is reaffirmed by the American women's traditions which from early times recognized the reciprocal impact of domesticity and public life. If these two are integrally connected, the woman movement realized, then women must help to shape society by developing a public voice which can speak of this ecology. This public voice needed to represent the changing concerns of women. As this voice became public, however, it risked representing privileged women to the exclusion of those women who must struggle to care for themselves and their dependents as best they can.

These traditions make different contributions to the problem of the exploitation of the poor. They point to the shared responsibility for care on all levels: national policy, local community concern, and family care. In their own time they reviewed international and national trade, national employment policies, and the practices of the professions, both in terms of the practices of lawyers and doctors and at the level of larger institution questions, such as the way institutions form character, for the ways in which they support or inhibit the family's quality of life. They recognized that women and children represent a group who are particularly liable to be without the necessities of life which put a quality of family life within reach. Only when these issues are addressed, can we retrieve the notion of individual self-sufficiency for the sake of psychic well-being.

Within a context of interdependent social practices, self-sufficiency can be conditionally reaffirmed. Self-sufficiency, as a partial ethic, is suggested when Luther writes, "the Christian is subject to none," and when Wesley suggests that "one cares for one's own necessaries." It is alluded to when feminists have argued *for* self-sufficiency for women. That is, a sense of relative personal self-sufficiency is psychologically necessary for all men, women, and children to develop a sense of power over their own lives. In as much as it contributes to a person's sense of individual worth, people need a realistic sense of self-sufficiency. Self-sufficiency becomes problematic when our sense of self-sufficiency denies our necessary interpersonal relationships and ignores the basic socioeconomic supports which for most of us are not provided by our self-sufficient efforts. Even political action on behalf of individual rights is never self-sufficient; it always requires the joint activity of at least a small political community which is willing to represent an individual's viewpoint. When, out of the denial of our essential interdependence, policy makers turn self-sufficiency into the primary norm of distributive economic justice, this obligation eradicates the possible psychic benefits of a personal sense of relative self-sufficiency because it denies the reality of the human condition. An ethic of care through shared responsibility allows room for the psychic empowerment of self-sufficiency by locating it within the larger context of interdependence.

Shared Responsibility in Public Policy

Theology contains some basic commitments which can guide the development of public policy, but public policy also carries within it its implicit theology. In *Poor Support: Poverty in the American Family*, David Ellwood demonstrates the kind of thinking which respects the reality of interpersonal and intersystemic interdependence. Ellwood suggests that deeper cultural values which are in touch with the ultimate commitments of Americans can become the foundation for American public policies. Ellwood's proposal for family policy provides an example through which I can illustrate how commitments in social policy can be consistent with religious commitments and meanings. While Ellwood claims to ground his proposal on general cultural values, the values he points to are civil religious values, in that they are ultimate commitments informed by a merger of religious and civic traditions. When these civil religious values are shown to have a genuine theological foundation, the Christian community will have grounds for supporting these kinds of proposals.

169

Ellwood has summarized the controversy over "values" among political conservatives and liberals.[3] Commentators on the politically conservative right, such as Charles Murray, have argued that the reason for increased poverty is a deterioration of personal values. The solution, according to the conservative thinking, is to create middle-class values in poor people by making them work. Political liberals generally argue that social systems, rather than individual values, have created poverty; therefore, the solution to poverty is social systemic change.[4] Ellwood has attempted to reframe the conservative-liberal debate over poverty by arguing for a comprehensive policy which is based on "American values" around which political conservatives and liberals could be united.

Ellwood begins his discussion by identifying four values which "seem to underlie much of the philosophical and political rhetoric about poverty." These values are "autonomy of the individual, the virtue of work, the primacy of the family, and the desire for and sense of community."[5] Ellwood states that Americans are most deeply committed to these values. While Ellwood does not use the term, the ultimacy Ellwood attributes to these values makes them "civil religious."

From a practical theological standpoint, one must ask not only *whether* values are a basis for public policy discussion but *how* certain values are grounded. "Autonomy of the individual" may be grounded in *laissez-faire* economics from which one claims that the individual's right to maximize self-interest is vindicated in the forces of the marketplace. Alternatively, "the autonomy of the individual" may be grounded in the Christian claim that the worth of every individual should be respected by the common community. "The virtue of work" may define work in the economic terms of capitalism and marxism in which valued work is paid, public work. Alternatively, "the virtue of work" may be grounded in the Lutheran sense of the God-given vocation of every individual in domestic and public work. "The primacy of the family" may be grounded in the right of fathers to govern their families which has been handed down from Greek philosophy. Alternatively, "the primacy of the family" may be grounded in the Wesleyan and Lutheran sense of economic and affective reciprocity in families which promotes the flourishing of children and adults. "The desire for and sense of community" may refer to a loose connection of volunteer interests which hopefully will happily complement one another. Alternatively, it may refer, as Wesley and Luther would emphasize, to the responsibility of the larger social system and its most powerful institutions to care for the most vulnerable persons it is supposed to serve.

In the conclusion to his book, Ellwood inadvertently shows the difficulty of maintaining civic values without turning to religious commitments. He describes an incident which Christians will recognize as theological. On the basis of this story, Ellwood's civic argument takes an unadmittedly theological turn. He argues that public policy for the poor must be based on *hope*. Ellwood quotes *New York Times* reporter William Geist; I quote them both at length.

> . . . sitting on the dais, Eugene Lang, multimillionaire industrialist, suddenly realized that the commencement speech he was about to deliver was complete balderdash, to put it nicely.
>
> He was about to tell 61 sixth-graders in a warm Harlem auditorium that he had also attended P.S. 121, a half century ago, that he had worked hard and made a lot of money, and that—quick, the No Doz!—if they worked hard maybe they could be successful too.
>
> Instead, Mr. Lang, a magnate with a no-nonsense style, stepped to the podium and told the graduates that if they stayed in school he would pay the college tuitions for each and every one of them: college educations on the house!

After describing the efforts of the parents, school, and Lang to support the children, Ellwood reports:

> For other students in this area, "dropping out is normal." As one student put it, "Around here, you are big and important if you drop out." Yet these students did not drop out. All of the 51 students who remained in the New York area are expected to graduate from high school, and 40 of them are expected to go to college. What is incredible is that Lang's offer to pay for their college education was not really necessary. Many got sizeable scholarships. And they all

171

could have gone to tuition-free or nearly tuition-free schools in the area.

It is obvious this is a unique and special story without any clear message for policy, since the government cannot create millions of Eugene Langs. But the story does offer something of a vision. What Lang seems to have offered these children was hope, along with services and direction.

Lang's act, like the parables of Jesus, creates a radical reversal of our normal expectations of behavior and reward. It reorients reality: instead of exerting power through bureaucracy and work obligations and lifestyle requirements, the person in the story who has power offers a free share in that power and the resources it can provide. As in the parables, some people make better use of that share than others. But regardless of their qualifications, all persons are invited to partake of the bounty. Jesus uses stories of such reversal to describe the relationship between God and humankind.

Such reversals are at the heart of theological narrative. The Hebrew Scriptures describe such social reversal as a regular public policy event. Every seventh year, the Jubilee year, the debts of the poor were forgiven. The Jubilee year echoes in the prayers of American Christians who routinely pray, "Forgive us our debts, as we forgive our debtors." According to Ellwood, Lang's modern Jubilee year worked with sixth graders in a public school in Harlem because it provided hope, one of the three theological virtues. According to Martin Luther, this free, radically reorienting, declaration of forgiveness and acceptance which calls for new social behavior, is God's grace which reveals human self-sufficiency for what it is. For Luther, the radical reversal creates faith. For Wesley, the radical illogic of God's prevenient grace is made manifest in interpersonal and socioeconomic relations through which faith is made perfect in love.

Implicit in Ellwood's foundation for public policy, beneath the civil religious values of autonomy, work, family and community, lies the theological offer of hope. Ellwood's decision to report this incident as he finalizes his argument points toward theological language as a language for reorienting our practice. Theological language helps us understand our deepest cultural commitments and provides a language with which to speak of those commitments. Therefore, one finds within public policy a skeleton of theological language. Shared responsibility, as an ethic of care, provides a relatively adequate theological skeleton upon which specific public policies for our time can be built.

Toward Transformative Practice: Public Policy Based on Shared Responsibility

Hope, faith, and love are concretized in the deep structure of Luther's and Wesley's ethics of care. Both theologians challenged the economic policies of the powerful: in Luther's case, the economically-based spiritual powers of Rome; in Wesley's case, the mercantilism and slave trade of Great Britain and the American colonies. Both theologians recognized that these national policies created conditions which impoverished women and children. Luther responded to this condition by developing an ethic of relational interdependence based on human need, the equal value of domestic work and public work, and accountability for the use of power. While criticizing national economic policies, Wesley recommended a radical levelling of family economics which promoted care for children. Furthermore, nations and neighbors are to care for poor families and individuals on the basis of "need." All families should have their minimal economic needs met. Furthermore, he recognized that psychological and economic security is necessary for basic character development which allows a person to become a contributing member of the community. He reminded the legal and medical professions that their vocation is in serving the community, rather than in lining their own pockets at the expense of the less fortunate. These fundamental values are echoed in the work of Ellwood and many of the thinkers upon which he bases his plan.

173

National Economic Policy

The theologians contended that the effects of national economic policy were felt most dramatically in the lives of the poorest people. This claim is echoed in modern social-scientific research. Therefore, macroeconomic policy proposals provide a context for more specific family assistance proposals.[6] Wilson argues that macroeconomic policies make the largest impact on poverty and determine the viability of family assistance programs. In terms of specific macroeconomic policies, he supports policies which continue to stimulate economic growth and which create a tight labor market. Noninflationary economic growth is necessary in order to avoid using unemployment as an antidote for inflation. A tight labor market is necessary to increase wages and to make affirmative action programs effective. From a theological standpoint, any specific macroeconomic policies must be tested by the conditions they create in the lives of the poorest people.

Household Economics

The theologians believed that the effects of economic policy resounded in the household. Therefore, each theologian built into his ethic an economic responsibility for the care of the family. Luther recalled fathers to the care of the family and neighbor, rather than to the spiritual pilgrimage. Wesley always included a phrase that one is responsible for the care of the neighbor "after the care of the necessaries of oneself and one's family." Neither theologian wrote those lines on behalf of the idolatry of the family or the accumulation of additional privileges for privileged families; rather, as a positive rather than limiting ethic, those lines become the theologians' "ethic of reasonable responsibility" for families.

This norm is consistent with Ellwood's contention that each family ought to have the opportunity to support itself. The descriptive reality which has been documented by Wilson, Weitzman, and Ellwood is that many American households cannot support themselves. According to Wilson's research, black inner-city families frequently cannot live up to this ethic because inner-city communities have disintegrated. He argues that black male unemployment may be the primary cause of the rise of the female-headed household in the black inner city. According to Weitzman's research, large numbers of women are also unable to live up to the norm of "caring for the necessaries of one's family." In many of these families, fathers could provide for their families but do not do it. The inadequacy of our national family policies allow fathers to ignore their child support responsibilities. The hidden bias behind women's inability to support their families reflects the low value we place on domestic work.

The Equal Value of Domesticity

Luther placed a great value on domestic work which contrasts with assumptions which ignore the economic and psychological value of domestic work. When one considers the value of domestic work, once must reconsider family policy in at least two ways. First, as in Weitzman's work, domestic work becomes a factor in economic equity for those divorced women whose children are fathered by an employed male. Second, domestic work is valuable to the family and to public society. The recognition of the value of domestic work to public society is at the center of European policies commended by Kahn and Kamerman, Weitzman, Wilson, and Ellwood. Sweden and France provide a governmental minimum allowance per child and state-collected child support. These European countries also provide monetary support for a custodial parent, as well as a policy of maternity leave for employed mothers. These countries do not talk of a "permanent underclass" or a "feminization of poverty."

Marriage and Children

Luther's anthropology led him to conclude that marriage was a lifestyle to be preferred over celibacy; Wesley, for the majority of his life, disagreed. Luther's anthropology led him to value the affective, sexual, reproductive, and economic life of human beings, all of which contributed to their vocation in the world as a vocation under God. Wesley was far more ambivalent about the extent to which marriage and "worldly business" could become Christian living. Despite these disagreements, both theologians' ethic of care for the poor, regardless of the circumstance of the poor, was a normative part of Christian living in a way that marriage was not. Both theologians held the family and the community responsible for the care of poor women and children, even though they looked to different institutions to solve the problem of "poor support." After providing for basic support which would make their care possible, Luther's anthropology would lead him to understand the desires of poor women to become mothers, and Wesley's anthropology would lead him to focus the attention of poor mothers on their response to God's grace which directs their contribution to the human community. For these reasons, they would reject a tradition which designates "deserving" and "undeserving" poor. Both theologians assumed that interpersonal patriarchy would be a part of Christian lifestyle, and it would be anachronistic to expect them to understand welfare mothers' claim that public assistance leads from "a man" to "the man." Despite their lack of understanding of systemic patriarchy, I conclude that their ethics of care would lead both theologians to be appalled at public policy which leaves so many unmarried women destitute. Likewise, Ellwood's proposal eradicates the distinction between the deserving and undeserving poor by supporting two-parent and all single-parent families equally.

Service and Profit in the Professions

Wesley placed a great value on the service motives of the professions, in contrast to the profit motives of the professions. In family policy, our modern form of this concern criticizes the professions of law and medicine. The divorce reform law was aimed at removing acrimony from the divorce process. This acrimony was fed by the profit motives of divorce lawyers who stood to benefit by couples' acrimony. Weitzman continues to support the intention of this law, even though she has warned about its consequences. All of the commentators have argued that the lack of adequate medical benefits for all people is one of the most impoverishing aspects of today's situation. Therefore, the profit orientation of the medical system, which provides luxurious and excessive care for some segments of the population while not providing even bare-bones care, such as affordable prenatal care, for the poor, would stand under the shadow of Wesley's criticism.

Character Formation

Wesley observed that the environment in which a person lives has a great influence on that person's character development. Therefore, it is important that a person's basic economic and relational needs are met. Similarly, Weitzman argues that parents and children have psychological needs which are related to economic stability.[7] Therefore, just as Luther argued that a neighbor should care for a neighbor based on the neighbor's need, Weitzman also argues that the needs of children and their parents should be the primary determinant in divorce settlements.

The Accountable Use of Power

Why are so many families unable to fulfill their basic needs? To answer this question the theologians would return to the issue of the accountable use of social power. Have we as a society exercised "reasonable responsibility" in the creation of social policy which makes the household responsibility possible? Just as Luther condemned the nobles for their exploitation of the peasants and Wesley condemned British and American national policies, the theologians would condemn us for not using our social power to create policies which make basic family subsistence possible. The theologians would not be content to let poor people "fall through the cracks." They would be outraged that we have not created social policies which repair the abyss created by the earthquakes in our present policies. David Ellwood's work suggests that the abyss into which poor people fall can be repaired if we have the will to do so. He has not only created a proposal of graduated care but has also addressed the economic issues of such a proposal. His work is built around a deep structure of interpersonal and social interdependence which assigns the individual, the family, and the government "reasonable responsibility" for self and other. In his proposal, the individual's "reasonable responsibility," like Luther and Wesley's theological ethic of interdependence, is based on the reciprocity between individual need and community contribution.

Ellwood claims that the largest group of impoverished households (nearly 50%) is female-headed, that the poverty of inner-city families is a quantitatively smaller problem but so extreme as to warrant special attention, but that the poverty of couple-headed families also illumines the problems of female-headed households. He argues that universalized programs can form an umbrella of social responsibility within which individual responsibility is possible. He creates this umbrella by attending to human need. He standardizes many of the decisions now made in the courts by providing governmental programs which allow for enforcement. Ellwood's proposals would significantly reform both welfare and divorce laws.

Ellwood suggests four problems areas which need attention in an effective program which eliminates poverty:

1. Two-parent families frequently remain poor with one parent working. They often have no medical protection and little governmental support. They suffer from temporary unemployment.

2. Single parents must balance the dual role of supporting their children economically and nurturing their children. This role balance often forces a choice between full-time work or welfare, and either choice disadvantages their children.

3. Absent parents often pay little or no child support for their children.

4. Families and children in the inner city experience extreme deprivation and little hope. They have few role models which can help them find a route to middle-class security. This insecurity and community breakdown often results in unproductive behavior, despite the best efforts of some parents.[8]

"Reasonable responsibility" includes both public and domestic work. Although Ellwood consistently uses the word "work" rather than "employment" to refer to paid work, he argues that families need half of their time for the care and nurture of children. In that way, he places an equal value on domestic and public work. He argues for the "family-wage" concept, saying that "in a two-parent family, the earnings of one person working full year, full time (or the equivalent number of hours of combined work by husband and wife) ought to be sufficient for a family to reach the poverty line."[9] A single parent, however, is held responsible by the same standard. She should be able to escape poverty by working half time. In essence, "reasonable responsibility" is for Ellwood the standard against which self-sufficiency is measured. Individual self-sufficiency is supported and made possible by a wide range of support services.

The theologians' concerns are echoed in Ellwood at their point of agreement that an individual's "reasonable responsibility" can only be exercised when society provides reasonable support. For Luther, society's reasonable responsibility for support requires accountability for the use of power. Ellwood's proposal, which we will examine in detail, is essentially a proposal for the just exercise of social power in today's conditions. A criterion for the responsible use of social power is whether our family policies are organized in such a way to make individual "reasonable responsibility" possible.

According to Ellwood, solving the problem of the poverty of couple-headed families is the first step toward eliminating poverty among single-parent and inner-city families. He proposes to:

Ensure that everyone has medical protection. Since the first loss for working families is medical insurance, an illness leaves a working poor family with medical bills they can never pay. Inevitably, the hospital industry absorbs these costs and compensates for them by raising the rates to paying patients. In that way, the public ends up paying for the medical costs of the poor. But poor families are severely penalized for these losses in ruined credit ratings and savings. These data suggest that national medical insurance is affordable.

Make work pay. Economic growth, through which wages and employment opportunities are improved, would be most helpful to poor two-parent families. However, the primary beneficiaries of economic growth would be couple-headed households. In addition, creating first-rate public schools in low-income areas would prepare better workers for the labor force. Both of these proposals will require longterm, consistent effort.

Ellwood suggests shorter-term proposals which would increase the value of low-paid work. He supports an increase in minimum wage as only a partial solution to the problem.[10] He suggests doubling the earned income tax credit and making the child care tax credit refundable.[11] These would be simple and of substantial value to poor working families. The present credit, which is not refundable and therefore of less value to the poor, "seems counterproductive, to say nothing of ethically troubling." He withholds judgment on further child care, saying that "whether the tax credit should be expanded ought to be debated in the much larger context of women's rights and the overall needs of children." He adopts the idea of a children's allowance from the European proposals, in the form of a refundable tax credit.[12] Ellwood estimates that increasing the minimum wage to $4.40 per hour and doubling the EITC would cost $6 billion and eliminate most poverty among the working poor.

Replace welfare and food stamps with transitional assistance of a limited duration. Provide a limited number of jobs for those who have exhausted their transitional assistance. Some reasonably responsible families would still be poor. A liberalization and expansion of unemployment insurance, education and training, and last resort jobs for that minority would provide a safety net for all of the poor who were willing and able to work and would virtually eliminate welfare.

Each of the labor market problems faced by the couple-headed family is exacerbated in the single-parent family. Labor market problems are compounded by gender bias in the labor market. According to Ellwood, however, what distinguishes the single parent family from the poor, couple-headed family is the "dual nurturer/provider role":

> Husbands usually work [*sic*] fully if they are not disabled. . . . Wives sometimes work [*sic*] fully but, more commonly, they work part time or not at all. . . . The provocative question is, Do we want single mothers to behave like husbands or wives? . . . By expecting single mothers to work part time, we would not be expecting them to behave like either husbands or wives."[13]

The most obvious and productive support for single parent families, according to Ellwood, is not workfare but child support. As in Sweden, the federal government should be responsible for assigning and collecting child support. He suggests three major steps to reform the present child support system.

> [1.] Society would commit itself to identifying every child's father and mother. In the future, the Social Security numbers of both parents would appear on a child's birth certificate. . . . What can be more difficult [than proving paternity] is finding the father years later if one does not have his Social Security number.

> [2.] All absent parents would be expected to contribute a portion of their income (earnings), and the portion would vary with the number of children they fathered or bore. There would be a roughly uniform formula for child support. For example, Wisconsin uses a plan that calls for 17% of the absent parent's income for one child; 25% for two children; and up to 34% for five or more children. Courts could deviate from the standard if the circumstances justified it.

[3.] In all cases, payments would be collected by employers just like Social Security taxes. . . . Employers would deduct the appropriate percentage of earnings just as they now do for taxes. The government would then send this money to the custodial parent. All absent parents would be included in the system, not just those who had been delinquent. The failure to pay would be an offense comparable to tax evasion.[14]

In addition to these proposals, which reorganize the present system, Ellwood supports Irwin Garfinkel's proposal for social insurance for children:

[4.] When the collections from the earnings of the absent parent were insufficient to provide some minimum level of child support, say $1,500 to $2,000 per child per year, the government would provide that minimum. In effect, when the father failed in his obligation to provide sufficient income for child support, the government would ensure that his children would get at least some minimum amount.[15]

Ellwood argues for this fourth provision on the basis of the idea that child support assurance represents a kind of unemployment insurance for children in homes in which one parent is absent. Furthermore, it provides a stable foundation on which single mothers can build. A mother could provide for her family with at least part-time work, and a father would know that he is fiscally responsible for any children he fathers.

Probably the weakest link in Ellwood's proposals for female-headed families is his "inability to evaluate the problems" of day care. He notes that many children are cared for by relatives, particularly their grandparents. Some day care operators say that money is allocated for day care that isn't spent.

Day care arrangements are difficult to evaluate, in my opinion, because the women who cannot afford professional day care find care in the "underground" domestic market. The underground market consists of those day care arrangements which are not licensed, and therefore, are not accountable to socially agreed upon criteria. Many children receive adequate care in the underground economy, but due to a lack of accountability, many do not. The underground market exists because domestic work, particularly child care, is undervalued as an economic activity. In the underground economy, the caregivers are often economically exploited, the children often receive reduced supervision and enrichment, and mothers are frequently desperate. Many women support their families through this underground market. While a day care tax credit is refundable, proposals for expanding support for home based day care centers, in particular, is important to any support proposal for female-headed families.

In addition, Ellwood's proposal does not resolve the problem of emotional parental absence. Increasingly, experts in the counseling professions agree that children need emotional access to both parents. The needs of children to have some contact with both parents are exhibited by adopted children who have gone to great lengths to find their biological families. In some divorced families, parents carry on their battles by non-payment of child support, which is countered by refusing access to children, or vice versa, with the children's needs caught in the middle. Federally-collected child support could collapse many of these battles. In addition, *parents*, rather than *mothers*, must be culturally recognized as caretakers of their children, regardless of family structure. Mothers must be supported, rather than scorned, when they share parenting with their children's fathers.

The genius of universalized care programs, such as those listed above, is that they care for all families while providing care for the poorest of the poor. Additional help for those in poor communities, in the form of community development rather than programs targeting individuals, is still needed. Ellwood suggests several areas of additional help for impoverished communities. First, education, particularly preschool education, is essential. Second, a longer school year would improve the learning of inner-city children. Third, work-study programs for older students might provide the job-networking which inner-city communities lack. Fourth, the poor can be empowered to keep control of their lives through education vouchers. Fifth, direct creation of jobs is expensive but necessary through both the public and private sectors.

Many commentators advocate teaching "values" to the residents of poor communities. Ellwood argues that values cannot be taught without a social system which rewards those values. At present, the deterioration of the inner city rewards an entirely different set of values, that of the underground crime and drug economy, and offers no real hope.

I have summarized Ellwood's proposals at length because they respond to many of the issues raised by analyses of gender, race and class; they are concrete, accessible to the laity of social science, and well-grounded. If Ellwood's proposals were enacted, Sidel's young women, in all three groups, could dream on, knowing that their ambitions in both domestic and vocational areas would receive the social support they deserve. Ellwood's proposals are grounded in reasoning based on a recognition of interdependence; in addition, they provide enough information that concerned people who have been largely unaware of this discussion will be able to follow and evaluate new proposals when they are made public. My hope is that the reader of this book will become confident as a co-thinker and discussion partner about poverty in the nineties, whether the discussion is conducted informally, across the kitchen table, or formally, in the church or association.

Few people can read any section of their Bible for very long without discovering the word that the care of the poor is the particular domain of God's people. In my experience, however, the church is very good at describing the problem of poverty but relatively poor in providing practical theological directions in which ordinary people can work. We know that we must work beyond emergency shelters, soup kitchens, and special offerings, but without information and concrete directions, the church's discussion of poverty results in guilt-tripping for the privileged rather than offering work for all to do. Many thinkers, identified in this book, have provided individual, social, and political directions to which church-people can respond. My goal has been to provide the theological reasons for doing so. People of material privilege, like the poor, need hope that something substantial can be done.

NOTES

Introduction

1. Data comparing single parenthood and family policies in European countries can be found in Alfred J. Kahn and Sheila B. Kamerman, eds., *Child Support: From Debt Collection to Social Policy* (Newbury Park: Sage Publications, 1988).

2. Charles Murray, *Losing Ground: American Social Policy 1950-1980* (New York: Basic Books, 1984).

3. Walter Lippmann, *Public Opinion* (New York: Harcourt Brace, 1922).

4. The practical as political incorporates ancient Greek and medieval meanings; the practical as personal refers to the growth of the idea of the *caritas*, or loving deeds, in the Christian era; the practical as technological is the modern idea which refers to skills, tools, and methods. See Nicholas Lobkowitz, *Theory and Practice: History of a Concept from Aristotle to Marx* (South Bend: University of Notre Dame Press, 1967).

5. For a discussion of thick description see Clifford Geertz, *The Interpretation of Cultures* (New York: Basic Books, 1973), 3-30.

6. Practical theological methods are necessarily fluid, depending upon the practice, situation, or habit being analyzed. The method I am employing is similar to that used in feminist or liberation theology and is close to that described by Don S. Browning in an unpublished manuscript, "Toward a Fundamental Strategic Practical Theology," and Rebecca Chopp in Lewis S. Mudge and James N. Poling, eds., *Formation and Reflection: The Promise of Practical Theology* (Philadelphia: Fortress Press, 1987), 120-38.

7. Note discussions of values in Kahn and Kamerman, *Child Support*, 363-363, and David T. Ellwood, *Poor Support: Poverty in the American Family* (New York: Basic Books, 1988).

Chapter 1

1. Peter Townsend, *Poverty in the United Kingdom*, quoted in Michael Harrington, *The New American Poverty* (New York: Penguin Books, 1984), 74.

2. Mimi Abramovitz, *Regulating the Lives of Women: Social Welfare Policy from Colonial Times to the Present* (Boston: South End Press, 1989), 77.

3. Linda Kerber, *Women of the Republic: Intellect and Ideology in Revolutionary America* (New York: W. W. Norton, 1980), 123–127.

4. Edward Shorter, *The Making of the Modern Family* (New York: Basic Books, 1975).

5. For example, in the period from 1900–1925, 70%–90% of lower-class black families were intact. William Julius Wilson, *The Truly Disadvantaged: The Inner City, the Underclass, and Public Policy* (Chicago: University of Chicago Press, 1987), 64–67.

6. Ibid., 199.

7. Heather L. Ross and Isabell V. Sawhill, *Time of Transition: The Growth of Families Headed By Women* (Washington, D.C.: The Urban Institute, 1975).

8. Wilson, *The Truly Disadvantaged*, 83-92.

9. Diana M. Pearce, "The Feminization of Poverty: Women, Work, and Welfare," *The Urban and Social Change Review* 11/1 (February, 1978): 28–36; and "The Feminization of Ghetto Poverty," *Society* (November-December, 1983): 70–73.

10. Barbara Ehrenreich and Frances Fox Piven, "The Feminization of Poverty: When the Family Wage System Breaks Down," in ed. Irving Howe, *Alternatives: Proposals from the Democratic Left* (New York: Random House, 1984), 162.

11. Ibid., 164.

12. Ruth Sidel, *Women and Children Last* (New York: Viking Books, 1986), 30.

13. Ibid., 25.

14. Diana M. Pearce, "The Feminization of Ghetto Poverty," 70–74.

15. Ruth Sidel, *On Her Own: Growing Up In the Shadow of the American Dream* (New York: Viking Books, 1990).

16. Ehrenreich and Piven, "Family Wage System," 163.

17. Pearce, "The Feminization of Ghetto Poverty," 71.

18. Sidel, *Women and Children Last*, 82-33.

19. Ehrenreich and Piven, 165. See also Sidel, *Women and Children Last*, 90.

20. Pearce, "The Feminization of Ghetto Poverty," 72. See also Sidel, *Women and Children Last*, 22-26.

21. Pearce, ibid., 73.

22. Kahn and Kamerman, *Child Support*, 15.

Chapter 2

1. John Kenneth Galbraith, "The Rush to Capitalism," *New York Review of Books* 37 (October 25, 1990): 51-52.

2. For a survey of women's changing domestic and employment patterns, see Kathleen Gerson, *Hard Choices: How Women Decide about Work, Career and Motherhood* (Berkeley: University of California Press, 1985). For cultural debates about the influence of feminism, see a collection of essays in Sanford M. Dornbusch and Myra Strober, eds., *Feminism, Children, and the New Families* (New York: The Guilford Press, 1988). For data on women, see Sara E. Rix, ed., for the Women's Research and Education Institute of the Congressional Caucus for Women's Issues, *The American Women 1987: A Report in Depth* (New York: W. W. Norton, 1987).

3. Gerda Lerner, *Black Women in White America* (New York: Pantheon Books, 1972), 620-621, contains an annotated bibliography of this literature.

4. E. Brooks Holifield, *A History of Pastoral Care in America* (Nashville: Abingdon Press, 1983).

5. Robert Bellah, Richard Madsen, William M. Sullivan, Ann Swidler, and Steven M. Tipton, *Habits of the Heart: Individualism and Commitment in American Life* (Berkeley: University of California Press, 1985).

6. Wilson provides an insightful analysis of the optimism in the liberal position toward civil rights in *The Truly Disadvantaged*, 6-18.

7. Daniel Patrick Moynihan, *The Negro Family: The Case for National Action* (Washington, D.C.: Office of Planning and Research, U.S. Department of Labor, 1965).

8. Harrington, *The New American Poverty*, 34.

9. President Johnson, quoted in Daniel Patrick Moynihan, *Family and Nation* (San Diego: Harcourt, Brace, Jovanovich, 1984), 31-33.

10. See Wilson, *The Truly Disadvantaged*, 148, on social pathologies.

11. For an analysis of sexism in the Moynihan report, see Paula Giddings, *When and Where I Enter: The Impact of Black Women on Race and Sex in America* (New York: William Morrow, 1984), 328-335.

12. Harrington, *The New American Poverty*, 22-35.

13. Sylvia Hewlett, *A Lesser Life: The Myth of Women's Liberation in America* (New York: The Free Press, 1985), 329.

14. Black women have been traditionally reluctant to adopt the aspects of feminism whose battle cry was women's independence from men. Historically, black women were alienated by early feminists who insisted that the problems of black women should be considered the domain of organizations concerned with race, rather than gender. In addition, black women recognize that black men have shared black women's economic insecurity but white women have not. Some contemporary black women have disassociated themselves from feminism because such goals as female independence are created from a position of privilege. Those black women who have named their position the "womanist" position have emphasized issues of economic justice over analysis of gender relations.

15. Wilson, *The Truly Disadvantaged*, 30-33.

16. In addition to *assuming* that most middle-class white female-headed households escape poverty, he recommends a tight labor market in order to make affirmative action more effective for black males. The slack labor market is helped, if not created, by the influx of women into the workforce; therefore, he may be implicitly suggesting that middle-class women are occupying jobs which could go to black males. However, he also argues for a policy of economic growth, and quotes Levy who attributes the economic growth of the 1970s and 1980s to women in the workforce. Wilson makes few systematic statements about women's work, although he does support "universalized care." Therefore, his position on women in the workforce, and what kind of a family policy is consistent with his macroeconomic proposals, is unclear.

17. Irwin Garfinkel and Sara S. McLanahan, *Single Mothers and their Children* (Washington, D.C.: Urban Institute Press, 1986), 15-17. On adolescent pregnancy, see Kristin A. Moore and Martha R. Burt, *Private Crisis, Public Cost: Policy Perspectives on Teenage Childbearing* (Washington, D.C.: Urban Institute Press, 1982). On the black family see Marian Wright Edelman, *Families in Peril: An Agenda for Social Change* (Cambridge: Harvard University Press, 1987).

18. A fine rendering of the interplay between divorced women's

economic decisions and their emotional concerns can be found in Judith Cassetty, *Child Support and Public Policy: Securing Support from Absent Fathers* (Lexington: Lexington Books, 1978); see also Terry Arendell, *Mothers and Divorce: Legal, Economic and Social Dilemmas* (Berkeley: University of California Press, 1986).

19. Lenore Weitzman and Ruth B. Dixon, "The Alimony Myth: Does No-Fault Divorce Make a Difference?" in *Family Law Quarterly* 14/3 (Fall 1960): 148-149.

20. The pitfalls of welfare reform legislation are described in Andrew Hacker, "How Fair is Workfare? Getting Rough on the Poor," *The New York Review of Books* 35/15 (October 13, 1988): 30-35.

21. Lenore Weitzman, *The Divorce Revolution: The Unexpected Social and Economic Consequences for Women and Children in America* (New York: The Free Press, 1985).

22. A summary of different kinds of distributive principles can be found in Michael Walzer, *Spheres of Justice* (New York: Basic Books, 1983), 3-30.

23. Warren R. Copeland, *Economic Justice: The Social Ethics of U.S. Economic Policy* (Nashville: Abingdon Press, 1988), 23-44.

Chapter 3

1. Ellwood, *Poor Support*, 132-133.

2. Plato, *Republic*, 5.451-5.455c.

3. Ibid., 5.455c.

4. Jean Bethke Elshtain, *Public Man, Private Woman: Women in Social and Political Thought* (Princeton: Princeton Univertsity Press, 1981), 35-41.

5. Plato, *Republic*, 10.614b ff.

6. Ibid., 10.615c.

7. Ibid., 10.604b.

8. An example of a work which makes this error is Susan Moller Okin, *Justice, Gender, and the Family* (New York: Basic Books, 1989). While Okin's premise that the family is the first teacher of virtue and her challenge to traditional ethical theory are to be commended, the work fails to interpret justice for women who lack social privilege.

9. Aristotle, *Nichomachean Ethics*, VIII.14.1163b.

10. Martha Nussbaum, *The Fragility of Goodness: Luck and Ethics in Greek Tragedy and Philosophy* (Cambridge: Cambridge University Press, 1986), 366.

11. Aristotle, *Politics*, I.1360a.

12. Nussbaum, *The Fragility of Goodness*, 240 ff.
13. Lobkowitz, *Theory and Practice*, 59-68; R. Newton Flew, *The Idea of Perfection in Christian Theology* (London: Oxford University Press, 1934), 151-145; Elizabeth Clark and Herbert Richardson, *Women and Religion: A Feminist Sourcebook of Christian Thought* (New York: Harper and Row, 1977), 53.
14. Elizabeth Clark, *Jerome, Chrysostom and Friends* (New York: Edwin Mellen Press, 1979), 16.
15. Ibid., 56, 17-18.
16. Ibid., 51.
17. Ibid., 165.
18. Lobkowitz, *Theory and Practice*, 59-63.
19. Clark, *Jerome*, 142.
20. Augustine, *De bono coniugali* 5.5., quoted in Peter Brown, *Augustine of Hippo* (Berkeley: University of California Press, 1967), 89, and Peter Brown, *The Body and Society: Men, Women, and Sexual Renunciation in Early Christianity* (New York: Columbia University Press, 1988), 393. Many interpreters of Augustine in the tradition of the psychoanalytic interpretation of religion have considered Augustine's choice of celibacy regressive, an oedipal defeat due to the overbearing influence of his mother Monika. I disagree with this line of thinking. Augustine does not complain about Monika's "clinginess" until after Patricius dies in Augustine's late adolescence when, significantly, Augustine needs Patricius to initiate him into the adult male world. Thereafter, Augustine's reflections are dominated by valiant attempts to come to grips with loss and disorder. Augustine's attachment to Christ represents what Ana-Maria Rizzuto, in *The Birth of the Living God* (Chicago: University of Chicago Press, 1979), 40, calls a "spouse-God," a mature form of relationship to God.
21. Brown, *Body*, 389.
22. Ibid., 387-427. See also Kari Borreson, *Subordination and Equivalence* (Washington, D.C.: University Press of America, 1981).
23. Jean Leclerq, *Monks on Marriage* (New York: Seabury Press, 1982).
24. Thomas Aquinas, *Summa Theologiae*, IIIa Suppl., Q. 49.
25. John Boswell, *The Kindness of Strangers: The Abandonment of Children in Western Europe from Late Antiquity to the Renaissance* (New York: Pantheon Books, 1988), 232-241, 256-266.
26. JoAnn McNamara, "Chaste Marriage and Clerical Celibacy," in eds. Vern L. Bullough and James A. Brundage, *Sexual Practices*

and the Medieval Church (Buffalo: Prometheus Books, 1982), 26-30.

27. James Brundage, "Concubinage and Marriage in Medieval Canon Law," in Bullough and Brundage, *Sexual Practices*, 118-127.

Chapter 4

1. Richard Wright, *Black Boy* (New York: Harper and Row, 1966), 22.

2. Luther, "Lectures on Genesis," *Luther's Works*, American Edition, ed. Jaroslav Pelikan and Helmut T. Lehmann (Philadelphia: Fortress Press, 1984), 7:18-50. Hereafter *Works*.

3. Lawrence Stone, *The Family, Sex, and Marriage in England, 1500-1800* (New York: Harper and Row, 1977), 154-155.

4. Lyndal Roper, "Luther: Sex, Marriage, and Motherhood," *History Today* 33 (Dec. 1983): 33-38.

5. Luther, "Disputation on Scholastic Theology," *Works* 33:12.

6. Luther, "To the Christian Nobility of the German Nation Concerning the Reform of the Christian Estate," *Works* 44:170-171.

7. This position may derive from Augustine. Augustine's criterion for "marriage" is loving faithfulness, rather than legality. See note 18 to Chapter 3, above.

8. From this beginning Luther will go on to develop the idea of the "common chest," an early distribution plan for parish-based caring for the poor. Luther criticizes early capitalism, especially the exacting of interest, which he finds incompatible with the practices of using one's money for caring for one another. For a summary of Luther's criticism of capitalism and experiments in early socialism, see Max Weber, *The Protestant Ethic and the Spirit of Capitalism*, trans. Talcott Parsons (New York: Charles Scribner's Sons, 1958), 79-92. See also Ernst Troeltsch, *The Social Teaching of the Christian Churches*, trans. Olive Wyon, 2 vols. (New York: Harper and Row, 1960), 2:562-576.

9. Luther, "To the Christian Nobility," *Works* 44:176.

10. Ibid., 178.

11. For an interpretation of Luther's understanding of relationality of the roles of men and women in marriage and in the church based on Luther's interpretation of the Magnificat, see Gerta Scharfenorth and Klaus Thraede, *"Freunde in Christus werden": Die Beziehung von Mann und Frau als Frage an Theologies und Kirche* (Gelnhausen, Berlin: Burckhardthaus-Verlag; Stein/Mfr.: Laetare-Verlag, 1977).

12. Luther, "The Judgment of Martin Luther on Monastic Vows," *Works* 44:264.

13. Luther, "The Freedom of a Christian," *Works* 31:307–326.

14. Luther, "On Good Works," *Works* 44:15–114.

15. In *The Social Teaching of the Christian Churches*, Ernst Troeltsch had noted the tension in Luther which disappears from later Lutheran theology. Troeltsch described Luther's critique of capitalism and his initiatives toward group social support, concluding, "when the social doctrines of Lutheranism are treated solely as the religious sanction of the existing situation, as often happens is orthodox Lutheranism, this always means that Lutheran thought has been weakened. . . ," 2:570.

16. Women sometimes look to the late Middle Ages as the time when work and home were ideally combined so that men and women could participate in what we consider "both spheres." The extent to which this was true seems to vary with geographical location. Compare the analysis of Lyndal Roper, *The Holy Household: Women and Morals in Reformation Augsburg* (Oxford: Oxford University Press, 1989) with that of Martha Howell, *Women, Production and Patriarchy in Late Medieval Cities* (Chicago: University of Chicago Press, 1986) who studied women in Cologne and Leiden.

17. Luther, "A Sermon on the Estate of Marriage," *Works* 45:17–18, and "The Judgment of Martin Luther on Monastic Vows," *Works* 44:351.

18. Luther's concern for relatedness has been ignored, in part, due to the misappropriation of the "two-kingdom theory" which developed in Lutheran scholarship. Bernhard Lohse, in *Martin Luther: An Introduction to His Life and Work* (Philadelphia: Fortress Press, 1986), 186–193, points out that the term "the doctrine of two kingdoms" was first used in 1922 by Karl Barth. The term eventually referred to a Lutheran doctrine, attributed to Luther, which argued for the "autonomy" of the church and the state. This misinterpretation of Luther is significant when it is called upon to support, first, a reactionary understanding of the "orders of creation"; second, an uncritical acquiescence of Christians to the rule of oppressive governments. Lohse, after summarizing the recent work of several scholars, including Gustav Toernvall, Johannes Heckel, Paul Althaus, Heinrich Bornkamm, Gerhard Ebeling, and Ulrich Duchrow, concludes that the doctrine of two kingdoms is built on two misinterpretations of Luther. First, the "kingdom of this world" is not limited to the state; therefore, the conflicts between two kingdoms cannot

be limited to a church v. state issue. For Luther, the kingdom of this world includes "the whole secular realm, including nature, the family, the arts, and all the sciences. The relationship of church and state is only one small section of this doctrine." Second, the two kingdom theory must include the idea of two governments of God, spiritual and secular, not only two kingdoms. When it includes the idea of two governments, the two-kingdom theory refers to two sides of a relationship between God and humanity, the spiritual and the secular, rather than referring to two ontological realities.

19. The original work on the idea of childhood as a distinctively modern concept is Phillippe Aries, *Centuries of Childhood: A Social History of Family Life* (New York: Alfred A. Knopf, 1963.)

20. Luther, "How God Rescued an Honorable Nun," *Works* 43:88-96. The revolt against monasticism began in 1521 with the marriage of several priests who adhered to Luther's writings.

21. Luther, "The Babylonian Captivity of the Church," *Works* 36:103-105.

22. Luther, "A Sermon on the Estate of Marriage," *Works* 45:20.

23. Luther, "How God Rescued an Honorable Nun," *Works* 43:81-96.

24. Luther, "Lectures on Genesis," *Works* 7:17

25. Alasdair MacIntyre, *A Short History of Ethics* (New York: Macmillan, 1966), 122.

26. Ibid., 121-122.

27. Luther's language of prostitution, which is not original with him, deserves attention. Some commentators consider Luther's language a psychological device which divides women into deserving and undeserving women; however, Luther is also following well-established rhetorical conventions. Earlier theologians, such as Thomas Aquinas, considered prostitution a necessary evil, using the now-famous analogy that "the prostitute is to society as the sewer is to the palace." See Vern L. Bullough, "The Prostitute in the Early Middle Ages," in Bullough and Brundage, *Sexual Practices*, 36. The reformers challenged that view and attempted to eradicate prostitution, initiating an understanding of sexual relationships as contributing to human relationality and procreation. This standard was to direct the sexual drives of both men and women. Although they blamed prostitutes for seduction, they were willing to undermine the economic tentacles of prostitution by providing prostitutes with the economic means to leave the brothel. For an alternative analysis of similar data, see Roper, *The Holy Household*, 1989.

28. Brian Gerrish, *Grace and Reason: A Study in the Theology*

of Luther (Oxford: Clarendon Press, 1962), 26.

29. Ibid., 16.

30. Ibid., 22.

31. Richard Sennett, *The Fall of Public Man* (New York: Alfred A. Knopf, 1977), 177-183.

32. Luther, "Treatise On Good Works," *Works* 44:26.

33. Ibid., 41.

34. Ibid., 51.

35. Ibid., 52.

36. Wolfgang Huber and Ulrich Duchrow have argued that Luther formulates the Christian life in terms of three statuses: the *status oeconomicus,* the *status politicus*, and the *status ecclesiasticus.* There is no hierarchy among them; all Christians participate in all three orders. Above the three statuses is the order of love which informs all three of them. It is a gift and a consequence of God's grace to fulfill good works in all these orders. The relational quality of human functioning in these orders is incorporated into Luther's idea of *cooperator Dei:* "those who work for God." Wolfgang Huber, *Kirche und Oeffentlichkeit* (Stuttgart: Ernst Klett Verlag, 1973), 440; Ulrich Duchrow, *Christenheit und Weltverantwortung: Traditionsgeschichte und systematische Struktur der Zweireichelehre* (Stuttgart: Ernst Klett Verlag, 1970), 502, 492 n. 195.

37. Luther, "Treatise On Good Works," *Works* 44:109.

38. Ibid., 111-112.

39. These charges are recorded by Luther in "An Admonition to Peace," *Works* 46:10-16.

40. Ibid., 19.

41. Ibid., 25.

42. Ibid., 36-37.

43. Erik Erikson, *Young Man Luther: A Study in Psychoanalysis and in History* (New York: W. W. Norton, 1958), 234-236.

44. Ibid., 52.

45. Luther, "Treatise On Good Works," *Works* 44:102.

46. For a description of the evolution of Lutheran domestic reforms, see Roper, *The Holy Household*, 58-61.

CHAPTER 5

1. Erikson, *Young Man Luther*, 52.

2. Thor Hall, "Wesley, Women and the Word," presented to the Wesley Studies Working Group, the American Academy of Religion, Boston, December, 1987.

3. For Wesley's dependence on early Christian platonism, see John C. English, "John Wesley and the Platonic Tradition," presented to the Wesleyan Studies Group, The American Academy of Religion, Anaheim, November, 1989, and English, "John Wesley's Endebtedness to John Norris," *Church History* 60/1 (March, 1991), 55-69. Ted A. Campbell, *John Wesley and Christian Antiquity: Religious Vision and Cultural Change* (Nashville: Kingswood Books, 1991) provides the best study to date of Wesley's understanding of and appeals to the paradigm of the early church. It is crucial to this chapter to distinguish between Wesley's platonic lifestyle and his aristotelian epistemology; for the latter, see Rex D. Matthews, *"Religion and Reason Joined": A Study in the Theology of John Wesley* (Th.D. Dissertation, Harvard Divinity School, 1986). In his dealings with his sisters, I contend that Wesley changes his mind about women in order to resolve the contradictions created by a "conflict of appearances," very similar to that described by Nussbaum in her section on Aristotle's method.

4. John Wesley to Susanna Wesley, 28 May 1725, *The Works of John Wesley*, Vol. 25: *Letters I, 1721-1739*, ed. Frank Baker (Oxford: Clarendon Press, 1980), 163. Hereafter *Letters I*.

5. Susanna Wesley to John Wesley, 8 June 1725, *Letters I*, 164-165.

6. John Wesley to Susanna Wesley, 18 June 1725, *Letters I*, 170.

7. Samuel Wesley to John Wesley, 14 July 1725, *Letters I*, 171.

8. Susanna Wesley to John Wesley, 21 July 1725, *Letters I*, 172-173.

9. John Wesley to Susanna Wesley, 29 July 1725, *Letters I*, 174.

10. John Wesley to Mary Pendarves, 19 July 1731, *Letters I*, 294.

11. John Wesley to Charles Wesley, 25 September 1749, *The Works of John Wesley*, Vol. 26: *Letters II, 1740-1755*, ed. Frank Baker (Oxford: Clarendon Press, 1982), 380-387. Hereafter *Letters II*.

12. Wesley, "A Thought on Marriage," *The Works of the Rev. John Wesley*, ed. Thomas Jackson, 3rd edition, 14 volumes (London: Wesleyan Methodist Book Room, 1872; reprinted Grand Rapids: Zondervan Publishing House, 1959), 11:465. Hereafter *Works*.

13. *John Wesley*, ed. Albert Outler (New York: Oxford University Press, 1964), 153. This tract supersedes his previous work, "A Thought on Marriage and the Single Life" (1743), for which he was criticized for spreading false rumors about marriage.

14. Wesley's position is striking in relation to Luther's since Luther at times argued *for* marriage on instrumental grounds.

15. John Wesley to Charles Wesley, 25 September 1749, *Letters II*, 380-387.

16. John Wesley to John Burton, 10 October 1735, *Letters I*, 442.

17. John Wesley to Martha Hall, 17 November 1742, *Letters II*, 90.

18. John Wesley to Martha Hall, 17 November 1742, *Letters II*, 90.

19. See letters from Ann Granville, Aug. 9, 1731, *Letters I*, 285 and 301; references to Aspernell and Clay in letter to Mary Wesley, *Letters II*, 456; compare to Clark, *Jerome*, 47. Lawrence Stone attributes the Lutheran Reformation's strengthening of patriarchy to the reinforcement of the male as the head of the household, particularly as spiritual adviser. While this may be true, the role of the male as spiritual and ethical adviser to women in monasticism had been well established. According to Clark, this model of friendship was taken from Cicero, although she notes the compatibility with both aristotelian and platonic views on friendship.

20. Clark, *Jerome*, 51.

21. Few people have ever written on Wesley's economic ethic, despite its prominence in Wesley's work. The American Methodist tradition, in particular, muffled Wesley's Tory political views and his criticism of American economic practice, especially the slave trade. Wesley was certainly not enamored of mercantile capitalism, but it is anachronistic and misleading to consider Wesley a socialist. As Theodore W. Jennings, Jr., points out in *Good News to the Poor: John Wesley's Evangelical Economics* (Nashville: Abingdon Press, 1990), Wesley did not advocate a system of state control of the means of production but presented theological criticisms of both socialist and capitalist systems. The existing works on Wesley's economic ethics appeared primarily during the time of heightened interest in socialism in the United States, as in Kathleen Walker MacArthur, *The Economic Ethics of John Wesley* (New York: Abingdon Press, 1936), or from authors with perspectives other than that of the U.S., as in John Wilkins Sigsworth, *World-changers: Karl Marx and John Wesley* (Stirling, Ontario: Easingwold Publications, 1982).

22. Wesley, "Thoughts on the Present Scarcity of Provisions," *Works* 11:53-54.

23. Wesley, "A Calm Address to Our American Colonies," *Works* 11:80-81.

24. Wesley, "Thoughts Upon Slavery," *Works* 11:67-68.

25. Ibid., 77.

26. Jennings, *Good News to the Poor*, 9.

27. Wesley, "The Late Work of God in North America" (1778), *The Works of John Wesley*, Vols. 1-4: *Sermons I-IV*, ed. Albert C. Outler (Nashville: Abingdon Press, 1984-87), III:594-608. Hereafter *Sermons*.

28. Albert Outler, "How to Run a Conservative Revolution and Get No Thanks for It," unpublished paper presented to the John Wesley Theological Institute, Northern Illinois Conference of the United Methodist Church, February, 1986.

29. Jennings, *Good News to the Poor*, 7, quotes Wesley, *A Farther Appeal to Men of Reason and Religion, Works* 8:133.

30. Jennings, *Good News to the Poor*, 48-69.

31. In "The Good Steward," and whenever he appeals for donations for the poor, Wesley writes: "but first supplying thy own reasonable wants, together with those of thy family; and then restoring the remainder to (Jesus) through the poor whom I had appointed to receive it." *Sermons* II:295.

32. Wesley, "The Danger of Increasing Riches" (1790), *Sermons* IV:184. The parenthesis, in this case, marks an assumed standard, rather than a secondary term. Compare, for example, another formulation from "The Good Steward" (1768), *Sermons* II:295: " . . . first supplying thy own reasonable wants, together with those of thy family; then restoring the remainder to (God). . . ."

33. Jennings, *Good News to the Poor*, 128.

34. Frederick E. Maser, *The Story of John Wesley's Seven Sisters, or Seven Sisters in Search of Love* (Rutland, Vermont: Academy Books, 1988).

35. Emilia Harper to John Wesley, 13 August 1735, *Letters I*, 430.

36. Emilia Harper to John Wesley, 24 November 1738, *Letters I*, 589.

37. Emilia Harper to John Wesley, 7 May 1741, *Letters II*, 99.

38. Ibid.

39. John Wesley to Emilia Harper, 30 June 1743, *Letters II*, 100.

40. Ibid.

41. Emilia Harper to John Wesley, 16 February 1751, *Letters II*, 449.

42. See the series of letters between Charles and John in June, 1755, in which they review their financial support of their sisters, *Letters II*, 560-563.

43. John Wesley to Ebenezer Blackwell, 4 February 1751, *Letters II*, 448.

44. Maser, *Seven Sisters*, 90.

45. Ibid., 94-94.

46. Ibid., 56-62.
47. John Wesley to Samuel Wesley, Jr., *Letters I*, 205.

Chapter 6

1. Ellen Key, *The Renaissance of Motherhood* (New York: G. P. Putnam's Sons, 1914.)
2. Thomas Jefferson, letter to James Madison, Oct. 28, 1785, *Thomas Jefferson: Writings* Library Of America (New York: Literary Classics of the United States, 1984), 840.
3. Ibid., 841.
4. Ibid., 841-842.
5. Jefferson, "The Autobiography," ibid., 44.
6. Abigail Adams, quoted in Rosemary Skinner Keller, "Women, Civil Religion, and the American Revolution," in *Women and Religion in America: The Colonial and Revolutionary Periods*, ed. Rosemary Radford Ruether and Rosemary Skinner Keller (San Francisco: Harper and Row, 1983), 392.
7. Ibid.
8. Kathleen Barry, *Susan B. Anthony: A Biography of a Singular Feminist* (New York: New York University Press, 1988), 14-38.
9. Ellen Carol Dubois, ed., *Elizabeth Cady Stanton/Susan B. Anthony: Correspondence, Writings, Speeches* (New York: Shocken Books, 1981), 63, 55.
10. Ibid., 67.
11. Ibid., 34.
12. Ibid., 88-101.
13. Ibid., 55-56.
14. Ibid., 91.
15. Frances Willard, *Glimpses of Fifty Years: The Autobiography of an American Woman* (New York: The M. W. Hazen Co, 1889), 609-610.
16. Ibid., 605-606.
17. Ibid., 613.
18. Frances Willard, *Women and Temperance, or The Work and Workers of The Woman's Christian Temperance Union* (New York: Arno Press, 1972), 242.
19. Jane Addams, *Twenty Years at Hull House* (New York: New American Library, 1960), 93.
20. Mari Jo Buhle, *Women and American Socialism 1870-1920* (Urbana: University of Illinois Press, 1981), 11.
21. Ibid., 39.

22. Nancy F. Cott, *The Grounding of Modern Feminism* (New Haven: Yale University Press, 1978), 41-49.

23. Ibid., 42-45.

24. Cicely Tyson, in *I Dream a World: Portraits of Black Women Who Changed America*, ed. Brian Lanker and Barbara Summers (New York: Stewart, Tabori and Chang, 1989), 27.

25. Melvin D. Williams, *Community in a Black Pentecostal Church: An Anthropological Study* (Prospect Heights, Illinois: The Waveland Press, 1974), 65. See also Arthur E. Paris, *Black Pentecostalism: Southern Religion in an Urban World* (Amherst: University of Massachusetts Press, 1982), 108.

26. Katie G. Cannon, *Black Womanist Ethics* (American Academy of Religion Academy Series, Number 60; Atlanta: Scholars Press, 1988), 4-5.

27. Ellen Key, *The Woman Movement* (New York: G. P. Putnam's Sons, 1912), 31-33.

28. Ibid., 3.

29. Ellen Key's critique of Christianity in her tract *Love and Marriage* (New York: G.P. Putnam's Sons, 1911), 12-17, contains specific reference to Luther. She recognizes the cultural inheritance Luther offers through his valuing of sexuality, suggesting, as I have argued, that Luther was influenced in his views of sexuality by the Renaissance and that he prepared the way culturally for the 19th and 20th century freethinkers. She rejects Luther, however, because in her opinion, his understanding of sexuality as a human drive leaves no room for an understanding of sex in relation to romantic love.

30. Buhle, *Women and American Socialism*, 292-294.

Chapter 7

1. Theresa Johnson, in the ABC special "God Bless the Children," produced by Bruce J. Sallan.

2. Sidel, *On Her Own*, 9.

3. Ellwood, *Poor Support*, 7-8.

4. Christopher Jencks reviewed *The Truly Disadvantaged*, in which Wilson identified "social pathologies" as a creation of the economic system, appreciating its scope but unconvinced by its disregard of values. Christopher Jencks, "Deadly Neighborhoods," in *The New Republic*, 198/24 (June 13, 1988): 23-32.

5. Ellwood, *Poor Support*, 16.

6. Wilson, *The Truly Disadvantaged*, 149-157.

7. Weitzman misreads the psychological needs of children at one

point, however. She bases her advocacy of a sole custodianship of a primary parent on a trade-off of economic and relational power between the parents. See Weitzman, *Divorce Revolution*, 393-395. She fails to adequately account for the need a child has for attachment to both parents. Although some research has suggested that a child needs a strong attachment to only one primary parent, I would consider that viewpoint a minority view. Most experts on children of divorce maintain the position that children thrive best when both parents put aside their conflicts with one another in order to maintain direct, supportive relationships with the child.

8. Ellwood, *Poor Support*, 232-235.

9. Ibid., 87.

10. Ibid., 112.

11. Ibid., 117.

12. Ibid., 118.

13. Ibid., 132-137.

14. Ibid., 163-164.

15. Ibid., 165.

SELECTED BIBLIOGRAPHY

Primary Sources

Addams, Jane. *Twenty Years at Hull House*. New York: New American Library, 1960.

Aristotle. "Nichomachean Ethics." *Introduction to Aristotle*. Edited by Richard McKeon. Chicago: University of Chicago Press, 1973.

Augustine. *The Basic Writings of St. Augustine*. 2 vols. Edited by Whitney Oates. New York: Random House, 1953.

Jefferson, Thomas. *Thomas Jefferson: Writings*. Library of America edition. New York: Literary Classics of the United States, 1984.

Key, Ellen. *Love and Marriage* (New York: G. P. Putnam's Sons, 1911.

———. *The Renaissance of Motherhood*. New York: G. P. Putnam's Sons, 1914.

———. *The Woman Movement*. New York: G. P. Putnam's Sons, 1912.

Luther, Martin. *Luther's Works: American Edition*. 55 vols. Edited by Jaroslav Pelikan and Helmut T. Lehmann. St. Louis: Concordia Publishing House, and Philadelphia: Fortress Press, 1955 ff.

Plato. *The Republic*. Edited by Richard W. Sterling and William C. Scott. New York: W. W. Norton, 1985.

[Stanton]. Dubois, Ellen Carol, ed. *Elizabeth Cady Stanton/Susan B. Anthony: Correspondence, Writings, Speeches*. New York: Shocken Books, 1981.

Wesley, John. *The Works of John Wesley*, Vols. 1–4: *Sermons I–IV*. Edited by Albert C. Outler. Nashville: Abingdon Press, 1984–87.

Wesley, John. *The Works of John Wesley*, Vol. 25: *Letters I, 1721–1739*. Edited by Frank Baker. Oxford: Clarendon Press, 1980.

Wesley, John. *The Works of John Wesley*, Vol. 26: *Letters II, 1740–1755*. Edited by Frank Baker. Oxford: Clarendon Press, 1982.

Wesley, John. *The Works of the Rev. John Wesley*. Edited by Thomas Jackson. 3rd edition. 14 volumes. London: Wesleyan Methodist Book Room, 1872. Reprinted Grand Rapids: Zondervan, 1958.

Willard, Frances. *Glimpses of Fifty Years: The Autobiography of an American Woman*. New York: The M. W. Hazen Co, 1889.
———. *Women and Temperance, or The Work and Workers of The Woman's Christian Temperance Union*. New York: Arno Press, 1972.
Wright, Richard. *Black Boy*. New York: Harper and Row, 1966.

Secondary Sources: Books

Abramovitz, Mimi. *Regulating the Lives of Women: Social Welfare Policy from Colonial Times to the Present*. Boston: South End Press, 1989.
Andolsen, Barbara Hilkert; Gudorf, Christine; and Pellauer, Mary, eds. *Women's Consciousness, Women's Conscience: A Reader in Feminist Ethics*. San Francisco: Harper and Row, 1985.
Arendell, Terry. *Mothers and Divorce: Legal, Economic and Social Dilemmas*. Berkeley: University of California Press, 1986.
Aries, Phillippe, *Centuries of Childhood: A Social History of Family Life*. New York: Alfred A. Knopf, 1962.
Barry, Kathleen. *Susan B. Anthony: A Biography of a Singular Feminist*. New York: New York University Press, 1988.
Bellah, Robert; Madsen, Richard; Sullivan, William M.; Swidler, Ann; and Tipton, Steven M. *Habits of the Heart: Individualism and Commitment in American Life*. Berkeley: University of California Press, 1985.
Bernstein, Richard J. *Beyond Objectivism and Relativism*. Philadelphia: University of Pennsylvania Press, 1983.
Borreson, Kari. *Subordination and Equivalence*. Washington, D.C.: University Press of America, 1981.
Boswell, John. *The Kindness of Strangers: The Abandonment of Children in Western Europe from Late Antiquity to the Renaissance*. New York: Pantheon Books, 1988.
Brown, Peter. *Augustine of Hippo*. Berkeley: University of California Press, 1967.
———. *The Body and Society: Men, Women, and Sexual Renunciation in Early Christianity*. New York: Columbia University Press, 1988.
Browning, Don S. *Practical Theology: The Emerging Field in Theology, Church and World*. San Francisco: Harper and Row, 1983.
———. *Religious Thought and the Modern Psychologies: A Critical Conversation in the Theology of Culture*. Philadelphia: Fortress Press, 1987.

Buhle, Mari Jo. *Women and American Socialism 1870–1920*. Urbana: University of Illinois Press, 1981.

Bullough, Vern L. and Brundage, James A., eds. *Sexual Practices and the Medieval Church*. Buffalo: Prometheus Books, 1982.

Campbell, Ted A. *John Wesley and Christian Antiquity: Religious Vision and Cultural Change*. Nashville: Kingswood Books, 1991.

Cannon, Katie G. *Black Womanist Ethics*. American Academy of Religion Academy Series, Number 60. Atlanta: Scholars Press, 1988.

Cassetty, Judith. *Child Support and Public Policy: Securing Support from Absent Fathers*. Lexington: Lexington Books, 1978.

Chodorow, Nancy. *The Reproduction of Mothering: Psychoanalysis and the Sociology of Gender*. Berkeley: University of California Press, 1978.

Clark, Elizabeth. *Jerome, Chrysostom and Friends*. New York: Edwin Mellen Press, 1979.

———, and Richardson, Herbert, eds. *Women and Religion: A Feminist Sourcebook of Christian Thought*. New York: Harper and Row, 1977.

Cloward, Richard A., and Piven, Frances Fox. *Regulating the Poor: The Functions of Public Welfare*. New York: Vintage Books, 1971.

Copeland, Warren R. *Economic Justice: The Social Ethics of U.S. Economic Policy*. Nashville: Abingdon Press, 1988.

Cott, Nancy F. *The Grounding of Modern Feminism*. New Haven: Yale University Press, 1978.

Dinnerstein, Dorothy. *The Mermaid and the Minataur: Sexual Arrangements and Human Malaise*. New York: Harper and Row, 1976.

Dornbusch, Sanford M. and Strober, Myra, eds. *Feminism, Children, and the New Families*. New York: The Guilford Press, 1988.

Duchrow, Ulrich. *Christenheit und Weltverantwortung: Traditionsgeschichte und systematische Struktur der Zweireichelehre*. Stuttgart: Ernst Klett Verlag, 1970.

Edelman, Marian Wright. *Families in Peril: An Agenda for Social Change*. Cambridge: Harvard University Press, 1987.

Eisenstein, Zillah. *The Radical Future of Liberal Feminism*. Boston: Northeastern University Press, 1981.

Ellwood, David T. *Poor Support: Poverty in the American Family*. New York: Basic Books, 1988.

Elshtain, Jean Bethke. *Public Man, Private Woman: Women in Social and Political Thought*. Princeton: Princeton University Press, 1981.

Erikson, Erik. *Young Man Luther: A Study in Psychoanalysis and in History*. New York: W. W. Norton, 1958.

Farley, Edward. *Theologia: The Fragmentation and Unity of Theological Education*. Philadelphia: Fortress Press, 1983.

Fiorenza, Elizabeth Schüssler. *In Memory of Her*. New York: Crossroad, 1983.

Fishkin, James. *Justice, Equal Opportunity and the Family*. New Haven: Yale University Press, 1983.

Flew, R. Newton. *The Idea of Perfection in Christian Theology*. London: Oxford University Press, 1934.

Fowler, James W. *Faith Development and Pastoral Care*. Philadelphia: Fortress Press, 1987

Frankena, William. *Ethics*. Englewood Cliffs: Prentice-Hall, 1973.

Furnish, Victor. *The Moral Teachings of the Apostle Paul*. Nashville: Abingdon Press, 1979.

Garfinkel, Irwin, and McLanahan, Sara S., *Single Mothers and their Children*. Washington, D.C.: Urban Institute Press, 1986.

Geertz, Clifford. *The Interpretation of Cultures*. New York: Basic Books, 1973.

Gerkin, Charles. *Widening the Horizons: Pastoral Responses to a Fragmented Society*. Philadelphia: Westminster Press, 1986.

Gerrish, Brian. *Grace and Reason: A Study in the Theology of Luther*. Oxford: Clarendon Press, 1962.

Gerson, Kathleen. *Hard Choices: How Women Decide about Work, Career and Motherhood*. Berkeley: Univeristy of California Press, 1985.

Giddings, Paula, *Where and When I Enter: The Impact of Black Women on Race and Sex in America*. New York: William Morrow, 1984.

Gilligan, Carol. *In a Different Voice: Psychological Theory and Women's Development*. Cambridge: Harvard University Press, 1982.

Harrington, Michael. *The Other America: Poverty in the United States*. New York: Macmillan, 1962.

——. *The New American Poverty*. New York: Penguin Books, 1984.

——. *Socialism: Past and Future*. New York: Little, Brown and Company, 1989.

Hewlett, Sylvia, *A Lesser Life: The Myth of Women's Liberation in America*. New York: The Free Press, 1985.

Holifield, E. Brooks, *A History of Pastoral Care in America*. Nashville: Abingdon Press, 1983.

Howe, Irving, ed. *Alternatives: Proposals from the Democratic Left*. New York: Random House, 1984.

Howell, Martha. *Women, Production and Patriarchy in Late Medieval Cities*. Chicago: University of Chicago Press, 1986.

Huber, Wolfgang. *Kirche und Offentlichkeit*. Stuttgart: Ernst Klett Verlag, 1973.

———. *Folgen christlicher Freiheit: Ethik und Theorie der Kirche im Horizont der Barmer Theologischen Eklärung*. 2nd. ed. Neukirchen-Vluyn: Neukirchener Verlag, 1985.

Jennings, Theodore. *Good News to the Poor: John Wesley's Evangelical Economics*. Nashville: Abingdon Press, 1990.

Kahn, Alfred J., and Kamerman, Shiela B. *Not for the Poor Alone: European Social Services*. Philadelphia: Temple University Press, 1975.

———. *Income Transfers for Families with Children: An Eight Country Study*. Philadelphia: Temple University Press, 1983.

———. *Child Support: From Debt Collection to Social Policy*. Newbury Park: Sage Publications, 1988.

Keat, Russell, *The Politics of Social Theory*. Chicago: University of Chicago Press, 1981.

Kegan, Robert. *The Evolving Self*. Cambridge: Harvard University Press, 1982.

Kerber, Linda. *Women of the Republic: Intellect and Ideology in Revolutionary America*. New York: W. W. Norton, 1980.

Krantzler, Mel. *Creative Divorce: A New Opportunity for Personal Growth*. New York: M. Evans and Company, 1973.

Lanker, Brian, and Summers, Barbara, eds. *I Dream a World: Portraits of Black Women Who Changed America*, ed. (New York: Stewart, Tabori and Chang, 1989.

Lazareth, William. *Luther on the Christian Home*. Philadelphia: Concordia, 1960.

Leclercq, Jean. *Monks on Marriage*. New York: Seabury Press, 1982.

Lefkowitz, Rochelle, and Withorn, Ann, eds. *For Crying Out Loud: Women and Poverty in the United States*. New York: Pilgrim Press, 1986.

Lerner, Gerda. *Black Women in White America*. New York: Pantheon Books, 1972.

Lippmann, Walter. *Public Opinion*. New York: Harcourt Brace, 1922.

Lobkowitz, Nicholas. *Theory and Practice: History of a Concept from Aristotle to Marx*. South Bend: University of Notre Dame Press, 1967.

Lohse, Berhard. *Martin Luther: An Introduction to His Life and Work*. Philadelphia: Fortress Press, 1986.

MacArthur, Kathleen Walker. *The Economic Ethics of John Wesley*. New York: Abingdon Press, 1936.

McCann, Dennis, and Strain, Charles R. *Polity and Praxis: A Program for American Practical Theology*. Minneapolis: Winston Press, 1985.

MacIntyre, Alasdair. *A Short History of Ethics*. New York: Macmillan, 1966.

Maser, Frederick E. *The Story of John Wesley's Seven Sisters, or Seven Sisters in Search of Love*. Rutland, Vermont: Academy Books, 1988.

Moore, Kristin A., and Burt, Martha R. *Private Crisis, Public Cost: Policy Perspectives on Teenage Childbearing*. Washington, D.C.: Urban Institute Press, 1982.

Moynihan, Daniel Patrick. *The Negro Family: The Case for National Action*. Washington, D.C.: Office of Planning and Research, U.S. Department of Labor, 1965.

——. *Family and Nation*. San Diego: Harcourt, Brace, Jovanovich, 1984.

Mudge, Lewis S., and Poling, James N., eds. *Formation and Reflection: The Promise of Practical Theology*. Philadelphia: Fortress Press, 1987.

Murray, Charles. *Losing Ground: American Social Policy 1950–1980*. New York: Basic Books, 1984.

Nussbaum, Martha. *The Fragility of Goodness: Luck and Ethics in Greek Tragedy and Philosophy*. Cambridge: Cambridge University Press, 1986.

Okin, Susan Moller. *Justice, Gender and the Family*. New York: Basic Books, 1989.

Outler, Albert C., ed. *John Wesley*. New York: Oxford University Press, 1964.

Ozment, Stephen. *When Fathers Ruled: Family Life in Reformation Europe*. Cambridge: Harvard University Press, 1983.

Paris, Arthur E. *Black Pentecostalism: Southern Religion in an Urban World*. Amherst: University of Massachusetts Press, 1982.

Pittman, Frank. *Turning Points: Treating Families in Transition and Crisis*. New York: W. W. Norton, 1987.

Poling, James N. and Donald E. Miller. *Foundations for a Practical Theology of Ministry*. Nashville: Abingdon Press, 1985.

Rix, Sarah, ed. for the Women's Research and Education Institute of the Congressional Caucus for Women's Issues, *The American Women 1987: A Report in Depth*. New York: W. W. Norton, 1987.

Rizzuto, Ana-Maria. *The Birth of the Living God*. Chicago: University of Chicago Press, 1979.

Roper, Lyndal. *The Holy Household: Women and Morals in Reformation Augsburg*. Oxford: Oxford University Press, 1989.

Rosaldo, M. Z. and Lamphere, L., eds. *Women, Culture, and Society*. Stanford: Stanford University Press, 1974.

Ross, Heather L. and Sawhill, Isabell V. *Time of Transition: The Growth of Families Headed By Women*. Washington, D. C.: The Urban Institute, 1975.

Ruether, Rosemary Radford. *Sexism and God-Talk*. Boston: Beacon Press, 1983.

——, and Keller, Rosemary Skinner, eds. *Woman and Religion in America: The Colonial and Revolutionary Periods*. San Francisco: Harper and Row, 1983.

Scharffenorth, Gerta, and Thraede, Klaus. *"Freunde in Christus werden": Die Beziehung von Mann und Frau als Frage an Theologies und Kirche*. Gelnhausen: Burckhardthaus-Verlag; Stein/Mfr.: Laetare-Verlag, 1977.

Sennett, Richard. *The Fall of Public Man*. New York: Alfred A. Knopf, 1977.

Shorter, Edward. *The Making of the Modern Family*. New York: Basic Books, 1975.

Sidel, Ruth, *Women and Children Last*. New York: Viking Books, 1986.

——. *Growing Up In the Shadow of the American Dream*. New York: Viking Books, 1990.

——. *On Her Own: Living in the Shadow of the American Dream*. New York: Basic Books, 1990.

Sigsworth, John Wilkins. *World-changers: Karl Marx and John Wesley*. Stirling, Ontario: Easingwold Publications, 1982.

Stone, Lawrence, *The Family, Sex, and Marriage in England, 1500–1800*. New York: Harper and Row, 1977.

Tracy, David. *Blessed Rage for Order*. New York: Seabury Press, 1975.

Troeltsch, Ernst. *The Social Teaching of the Christian Churches*. Tr. Olive Wyon. 2 volumes. New York: Harper and Row, 1960.

Walzer, Michael. *Spheres of Justice*. New York: Basic Books, 1983.

Weber, Max. *The Protestant Ethic and the Spirit of Capitalism*. Translated by Talcott Parsons. New York: Charles Scribner's Sons, 1958.

Weinreb, Lloyd. *Natural Law and Justice*. Cambridge: Harvard University Press, 1987.

Weitzman, Lenore. *The Divorce Revolution: The Unexpected Social and Economic Consequences for Women and Children in America*. New York: The Free Press, 1985.

Williams, Melvin D. *Community in a Black Pentecostal Church: An Anthropological Study*. Prospect Heights, Illinois: The Waveland Press, 1974.

Wilson, William Julius. *The Declining Significance of Race*. Chicago: University of Chicago Press, 1980.

——. *The Truly Disadvantaged: The Inner City, the Underclass, and Public Policy*. Chicago: University of Chicago Press, 1987.

Secondary Sources: Periodicals

Carr, Anne, and Fiorenza, Elizabeth Schüssler. "Women, Work, and Poverty." *Concilium* 194. Edinburgh: T & T Clark, 1987.

Cole, Charles, ed. "Fundamentalism and Politics." *Quarterly Review* 4/2 (Summer 1984).

Franklin, Donna L. "Race, Class and Adolescent Pregnancy: An Ecological Analysis." *American Journal of Orthopsychiatry* 58/3 (July, 1988): 339–354.

Galbraith, John Kenneth. "The Rush to Capitalism." *New York Review of Books* 37 (October 25, 1990): 51–52.

Hacker, Andrew. "How Fair is Workfare? Getting Rough on the Poor." *The New York Review of Books* 35/15 (October 13, 1988): 30–35.

Hopper, Pauline and Zigler, Edward. "The Medical and Social Science Basis for a National Infant Care Leave Policy." *American Journal of Orthopsychiatry* 58/3 (July, 1988): 324–338.

Jencks, Christopher. Review of *The Truly Disadvantaged*. *The New Republic* 198/24 (June, 1988): 23–32.

McIsaac, Hugh. Review of *The Divorce Revolution*. *Conciliation Courts Review* 24/1 (June, 1986): 127–129.

Pearce, Diana M. "The Feminization of Poverty: Women, Work, and Welfare." *The Urban and Social Change Review* 11/1 (February, 1978): 28–36.

———. "The Feminization of Ghetto Poverty." *Society* (November–December, 1983): 70–73.

Roper, Lyndal. "Luther: Sex, Marriage, and Motherhood." *History Today* 33 (Dec. 1983): 33–38.

Weitzman, Lenore. "The Economics of Divorce: Social and Economic Consequences of Property, Alimony, and Child Support Awards." *UCLA Review* 28/6 (August, 1981): 1181–1268.

———, and Dixon, Ruth B. "The Alimony Myth: Does No-Fault Divorce Make a Difference?" *Family Law Quarterly* 14/3 (Fall 1960): 148–149.

Secondary Sources: Unpublished Manuscripts

Browning, Don S. "Toward a Fundamental Strategic Practical Theology." Privately circulated.

English, John C. "John Wesley and the Platonic Tradition." Presented to the Wesleyan Studies Group, The American Academy of Religion, Anaheim, November, 1989.

Hall, Thor. "Wesley, Women, and the Word." Presented to the Wesleyan Studies Group, The American Academy of Religion, Boston, December, 1987.

Matthews, Rex D. *"Religion and Reason Joined": A Study in the Theology of John Wesley*. Th.D. Dissertation, Harvard Divinity School, 1986.

Outler, Albert C. "How to Run a Conservative Revolution and Get No Thanks for It." Presented to the John Wesley Theological Institute, Northern Illinois Conference of the United Methodist Church, February 11, 1986.